# FROM BIRTH TO THREE

An Illustrated Journey Through Your Child's Early Physical and Emotional Development

Camilla Jessel

**Delta**

A Delta Book
Published by
Dell Publishing
a division of
Bantam Doubleday Dell Publishing Group, Inc.
666 Fifth Avenue
New York, New York 10103

This work was first published in Great Britain by Bloomsbury
Publishing Limited.

Library of Congress Cataloging in Publication Data

Jessel, Camilla.
From birth to three: an illustrated journey through your child's
early physical and emotional development / Camilla Jessel.
p.    cm.
ISBN 0-385-30310-6 (pbk.): 12.95
1. Child development – Pictorial works. 2. Infants –
Development – Pictorial works. I. Title.
HQ781.5.J47 1991
305.23'2'0222-dc20                                    90-13864
                                                         CIP

Printed in Singapore by Imago Publishing Limited
First U.S.A. printing

April 1991

10   9   8   7   6   5   4   3   2   1

Designed by Marnie Searchwell

# CONTENTS

## BIRTH

## PHYSICAL DEVELOPMENT

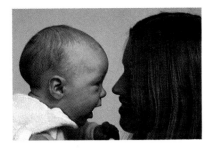

# EMOTIONAL GROWTH

# SPEECH

# PLAY

# RELATIONSHIPS WITH OTHER CHILDREN

# FIRST MOMENTS

In the womb your baby experiences unruffled, comfortable sameness. The temperature around her is always just right. Effortlessly, she absorbs all the oxygen and food she requires and eliminates her wastes through the umbilical cord.

The birth process is inevitably a shock as she is plunged from all-embracing calm into the increasing pressure of thudding contractions – the squeezing and the strain of being born. As she finally emerges, suddenly she has to use her own lungs to breathe, as well as to adjust to cool air around her, to light and sound and touch.

The baby may be sleepy after delivery, especially if her mother has needed heavy sedation. Or she may quickly be wide awake, not only ready for the first feed, but instinctively fixing her regard on a human face rather than anything else that she sees in her first moments.

This innate ability to select what she looks at comes from way back in evolution. She is beginning to learn to recognize her own mother: an 'imprinting' instinct similar to that of a young bird, who must (more rapidly) know its own parent for safety within a flock.

Your baby is also pre-programmed to fix her attention on a human voice, especially one of higher, female tones. (Some researchers believe that infants respond more to their mothers' voices as they have heard similar sound patterns from within the womb.)

*Though the labour was straightforward, Lee's birth was alarming. His father watched as he emerged into the world: a glimpse of dark hair, a little wrinkled brow, the eyes, the nose – but then – the cord was round his neck, almost strangling him! The midwife snipped with ice-cool speed. For many minutes, instead of lying comfortably close to his proud mother, the tiny, spraddled blue figure fought for his life on a resuscitating machine.*

*Then the fright was over. Lee began to breathe by himself and a pink flush swept away the blue.*

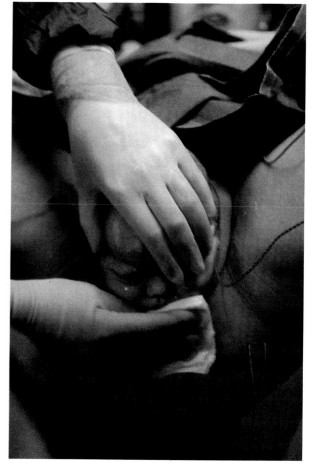

With trauma safely in the past, the room was darkened, and he was in his mother's arms, struggling to open his eyes. His instinct to look about him was stronger than the discomfort of his first experience of light. He immediately fixed his glance on the face closest to his.

His father exclaimed in amazement at his look of curiosity and the steadiness of his stare. Lee seemed to listen to his voice, turning his ear then tracking with his eyes towards the source of the sound.

# INBORN SURVIVAL SKILLS

Your new baby seems physically helpless, yet she is well equipped for survival. From the moment of birth she can begin to suck, feed and eliminate wastes, to cry and tell you of her discomfort. Her taste-buds will be adjusted for colostrum, the sweet liquid which comes through before breast milk, filled with your precious antibodies against disease. She will accept a bottle of similar flavour, but if given anything sour or salty, she will, right from birth, wrinkle her face with disgust.

She is born with several reflex responses, some of them useful, others just curious left-overs from an earlier stage in our evolution.

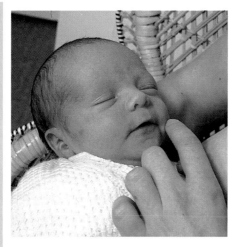

*At first Lee could do nothing on purpose: he could only react to stimulus. He could not decide to open his mouth ready for a feed, but a touch on the cheek – even an accidental one from a toy – would evoke a reflex to separate his lips and set him rooting for a nipple. Bottle or breast against his lips could then activate a sucking reflex.*

*He had many other reflexes, some life-saving, others not much use to human babies today, but traceable in their origins back to our hairier ancestors whose babies had to hold on tight as they leapt from tree to tree.*

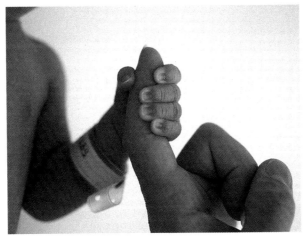

Lee's grip reflex was so strong that he could for a moment support his own weight.

Even from birth he could not help grasping anything that touched the insides of his fingers, and he could not voluntarily release his grip, which was so tight that the tips of his fingers turned white as the blood ran from them. He could also grasp with his toes, or spread them wide as fingers if the sole of his foot was stroked.

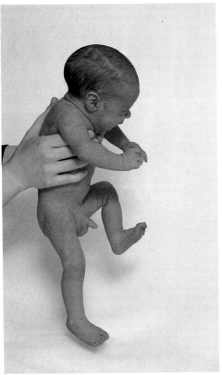

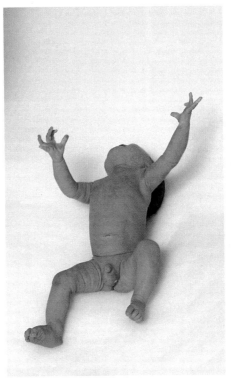

If his feet were trailed over a flat surface, suddenly he would start to lift his feet one in front of the other in an impressive walking action.

If startled by a loud sound or sudden movement, he would throw back his arms as if preventing himself from falling, then bring his hands back together as if trying to clutch on to something.

A bright light made him blink, and he reacted sharply to pain, using his fist or his foot to kick anything that hurt him.

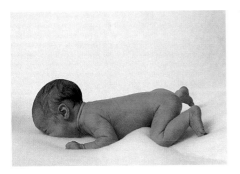

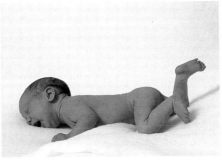

An effective life-saving reflex was his inborn ability to push away anything that came over his mouth and nose.

Laid face down, in spite of the weakness and floppiness of his body and the disproportionate weight of his head, he would automatically turn to the side so that he wouldn't suffocate.

# UNCURLING INTO ACTION

The first month or so represents an interim stage between foetus and active infant. Movements are jerky and mostly purposeless. Little by little your baby will work her way into co-ordinating her movements, exercising her body by kicking and wriggling and will soon be ready to reach out both physically and mentally.

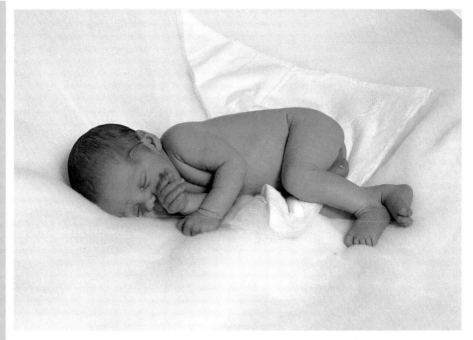

*Two weeks*

*For the first two or three weeks Lee continued to fold back sleepily into his foetal position. He was not yet co-ordinated enough to reach out to touch anything. And when his hand arrived at his mouth (on autopilot), he could not separate one finger to suck, but would chomp for comfort on his whole fist.*

Gradually his back straightened but still he could not move his limbs freely: when the arm and leg of one side were extended, the limbs of the opposite side bent upwards to hold his balance. (This is known to child experts as the 'fencer's position'.)

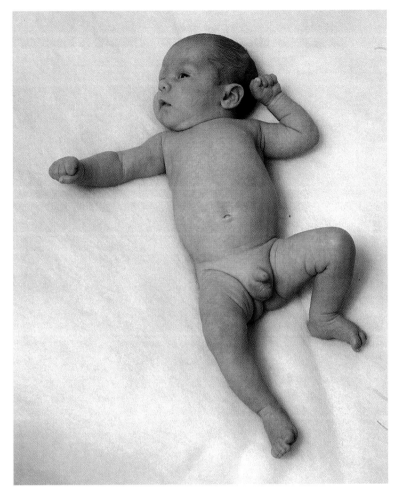

*Three and a half weeks*

However, he soon became more supple and lithe. At four or five weeks he could move his head and look about him. He could kick his legs quite energetically and appeared to be almost ready to reach out for an object of interest.

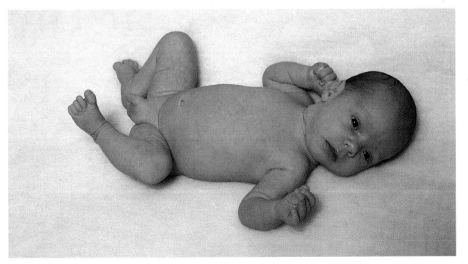

*Four and a half weeks*

# STRENGTHENING NECK

At birth, your baby's head is roughly one-third of her total volume: an overwhelming weight in comparison with her floppy, curled-up body. Her strength and her movement will start developing in her neck and will gradually progress down her spine, hips and legs.

She will probably double her weight in her first half-year. If she were to continue to grow at this rate for the rest of her childhood, she would be the size of three average adults by the time she was three years old, of more than fifty thousand adults by the time she was ten, and of about three and a half billion adults by the time she was eighteen!

*Laid on his stomach, for the first two or three weeks, Lee could hardly lift his heavy head. But curiosity is an in-built instinct, and he struggled to look about him.*

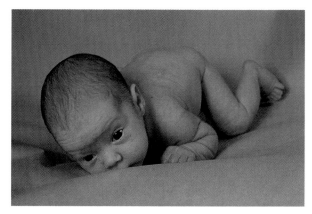

*Slowly his neck muscles began to gain strength: he would hold up his head for a moment, then it would drop like a plumb-stone, and bob up as he tried again.*

*Different babies develop this strength at widely different speeds. Edward, Lee's 'twin', born on the same day at the same hospital, could straighten his arms and hold his head higher and more steadily at six weeks.*

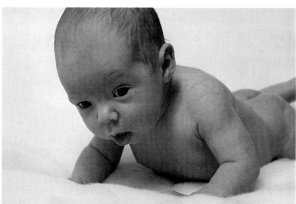

*However, at seven weeks, Lee seemed the stronger as he was able to hold his head upright while in a sitting position. At first he could do this for only a couple of seconds before gravity took over and his head bobbed backwards.*

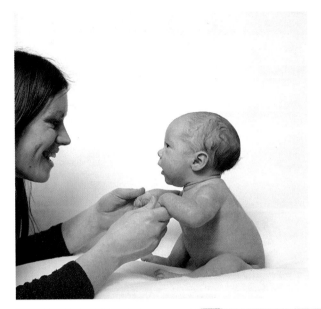
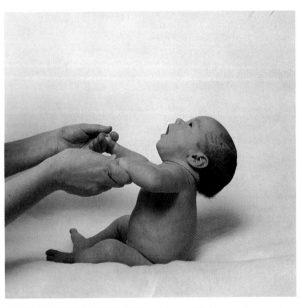

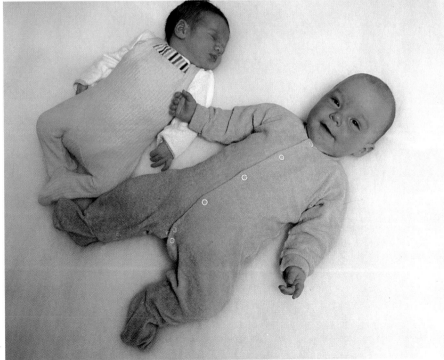

*Meanwhile he was also growing extremely fast. At twenty-two weeks he looked like a giant beside his two-week-old cousin Suki (who had weighed one pound more than him at birth).*

# CO-ORDINATING HANDS WITH EYES

Your baby has an innate knowledge of how to grasp, and the sort of objects she wants to get hold of.

However, she has to practise for several weeks not only to learn the length of her arm, but also how to move it accurately, so that her hand ends up in the right place. Information like this cannot be passed down genetically as tall and short babies will have arms of different lengths.

*From his first week, certain objects around the house attracted Lee's attention, especially those in bright colours and with patterns. Though he could not yet manage to touch them, he seemed to reach out with his eyes, his body tense with interest.*

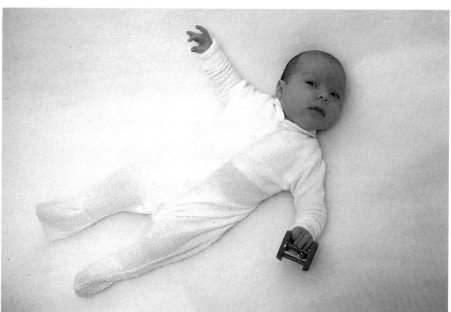

*At around three or four weeks, though his grasp reflex caused him to hold on to a rattle, he had neither balance nor co-ordination enough to bring it into his sight-line.*

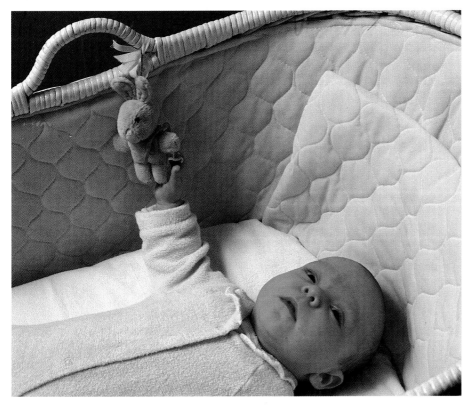

*Between eight and ten weeks, his sight was still not co-ordinating properly with his hand movements. Though he sometimes found himself touching his rabbit without looking at it he almost always missed when he took a purposeful swipe.*

*As his aim became more co-ordinated, he tried carefully to catch hold of any attractive object placed within his sight range. But this was not so easy. He had to master timing as well as distance; and his fingers would snap shut either before he'd reached it or after he'd already missed.*

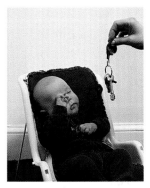

*His mother tried to help him practise his grabbing skills, hoping he'd catch up with friend Edward, who, as usual, seemed to be ahead of Lee in these achievements. But it was pointless to rush him. He needed to work through each developmental stage in his own time, without even the faintest pressure from his mother; he would become quite distressed or would switch off if his mother asked something of him that he couldn't quite understand.*

Physical development
# TAKING HOLD

Man the tool-user doesn't achieve his pre-eminence over other creatures too easily. It will take your baby many months to work through from utter helplessness to being able to take hold of an object and manipulate it with some control and skill.

*At two and a half months, Lee still had real problems bringing a rattle accurately to his mouth. All too often, he biffed his nose or his eye, yet instinct plus desire made him practise time and again.*

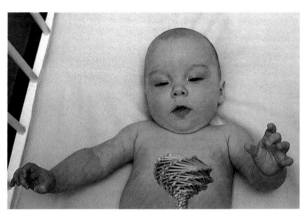

*Measure . . .*

*Miss . . .*

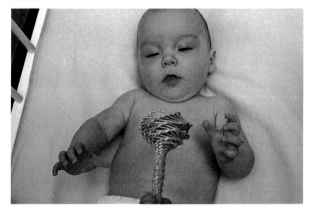

*Measure . . .*

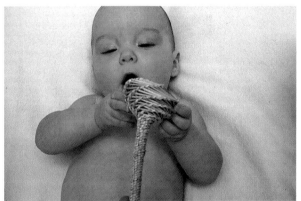

*Success!*

*Accurate grasping was still a matter for careful study. Using both hands, looking from the rattle to his hands and back to the rattle again, he tried and tried until he triumphed.*

*Neither could he cope with two objects at once: if a second rattle was put into his hand, his attention lapsed from the first and he would involuntarily drop it.*

*If helped to hold on to two objects at the same time, he got in a hopeless muddle.*

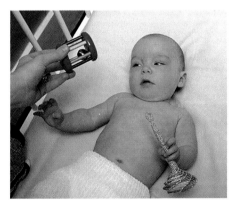

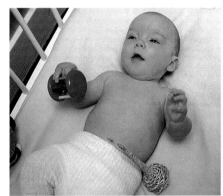

# INCREASING STRENGTH AND MOVEMENT

*Gradually Lee's body became firmer and stronger. No longer just flopped into his baby chair, he now could look around the room from corner to corner for his essential daily learning-through-staring; while, with his improved balance, his arms as well as his hands were free to play.*

*Lying awake in his cot, he would kick energetically and happily, further strengthening his spine, hips and knees. By three and a half months, he was already taking his weight on his feet, using his mother as a springboard.*

*Lithe and active in her arms, he suddenly became a 'grabber' rather than just a 'looker'. Now she had always to be alert since he had no concept of danger.*

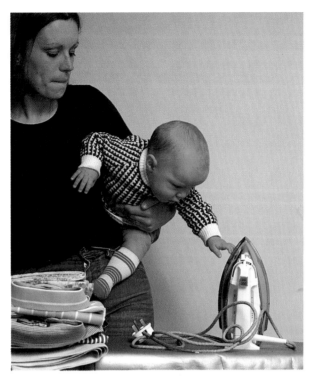

*On the floor he also soon became much more mobile. At about five months, he could turn over from his side on to his stomach; only a week later, he achieved a full roll from his back on to his front.*

*At six months he could sometimes reach out for a toy by twisting and slithering towards it. However, to his frustration, the more he tried to propel himself forwards, the more his awkward pre-crawl efforts seemed to drag him backwards, further and further away from the object of his desire.*

# THE SITTER

*At around eight months, Lee still could not sit on his own. His mother kept setting him into the right position, but he always flopped sideways or forwards. His frame simply was not ready.*

*He himself was perfectly happy, not knowing what he was missing. He had plenty to do: practising looking backwards over his shoulder, lifting his head to see his feet, pushing himself up on his forearms, placing his head face downwards and lifting his behind in the air and all sorts of other developmental acrobatics.*

*At last he managed to stay put . . .*

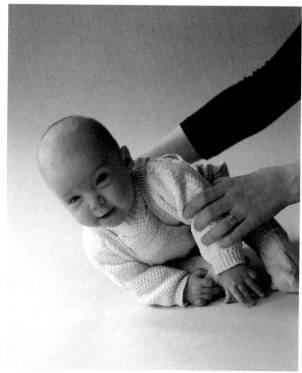

*. . . for a moment . . .*

*It didn't take long for his balance
to become steady, especially when
he became so absorbed with a toy
that he forgot the problem of
staying upright.*

*Sitting was a tremendous asset.
His arms were no longer occupied
in holding him steady;
exploration and play could now
take place from a firm base.*

# PRE-CRAWLING

Watch out for that forward-reaching movement. It means that your baby is almost ready for take-off.

Don't hurry her progress. Enjoy her comparative immobility. These will be the last moments that you can put her on the floor without having to worry too much about dangers around the house. Now is the time to check fire-guards and buy safety caps for electrical sockets.

Only too soon, not only will she be exploring those clean, sensible objects that you choose to put into her hands, but she will also be looking seriously into everything she can see: she will take an intelligent interest in the dog's dinner, she will pick up your outdoor shoes for a good chew, explore electrical wires with her mouth and try her newly acquired hand-skills on the lid of the bleach bottle.

She is going to be into *everything*.

*Before long, Lee could sit and concentrate for a full half-hour without tiring. However, when the object of his momentary passion fell out of reach, he was miserably frustrated . . .*

*Just a few days later, however, he had mustered enough balance and confidence to reach out further, then safely to regain his comfortable sitting-working position. With that forward-extended stretch, he was pretty well poised to crawl. Now he had only to turn his feet back under his knees and he would be away.*

# CRAWLING – THE TAKE-OFF

*Almost crawling – almost – but somehow one foot kept getting in the way!*

*After more days of puzzled struggle, suddenly he was sprung for take-off . . .*

*. . . at first moving more like a puppy than a baby . . .*

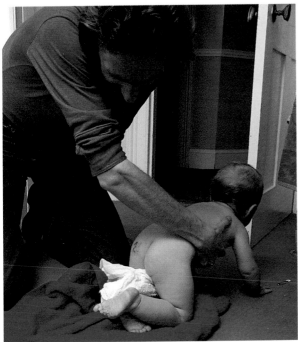

*Soon he got his knees to the ground; then there was no stopping him, escaping from a nappy-change or finding his way into the cat-basket.*

# PULLING UP TO STANDING

*Within days of being able to crawl, Lee was pulling himself up to standing. He didn't make any effort to walk: he seemed quite happy to crawl to any desired point of exploration and then pull himself up. Now he was exploring everything, and the dangers around the home were multiplied tenfold.*

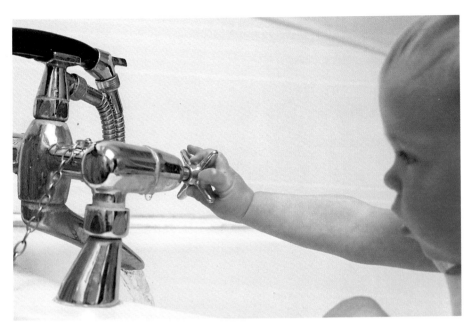

*He became expert at turning television knobs or dangerous hot taps; his hand-skills were improving faster than his balance on his legs.*

*His mother had not listened to warnings that she should accustom him to a play-pen before he discovered mobility. Having tasted freedom, he roared at restraint.*

# WALKING AT LAST

From four or five months, your baby will enjoy flexing her legs and looking about her (for short periods at a time) from the vantage point of a baby-bouncer. Once she is firm on her feet, she may enjoy a brick truck or a framed walker, which may well speed her progress on to solo staggering.

If she's forward in walking, she'll have a marvellous time rushing into all sorts of exploration and mischief. If she's slower to take off, don't worry. She gets where she wants all too easily by crawling, and learns more about safety from floor level. Also keep in mind that baby development is not a race: no one will remember as time passes whether your friend's baby or yours reached the milestones first.

Your baby might walk alone before she's a year old, or she might take until she's almost two. Research has shown that early or late walking makes no difference in the long run with regard to eventual prowess in sport or in anything else. Early walkers have such a good time hurtling about that they are sometimes later in learning to talk, but this also evens up in due course.

*From five months, Lee cavorted in his bouncer, visibly strengthening his legs. Perhaps he was going to be an exceptionally early walker.*

*At seven months, when held upright, he could stride along, throwing one foot in front of the other, apparently on the verge of walking before he could crawl. His proud parents felt they had hatched an athlete. However, it took almost another whole year before he could walk alone!*

*At ten months he 'cruised' around a room, leaning on furniture and stepping sideways. At twelve months, with one hand held by an adult, he could walk forwards as well as laterally. He could also walk several yards supported by his brick truck.*

At thirteen months, on seeing his mother's handbag across the room, intent on a demolition job, he suddenly took off into space – but sank as he sensed the lack of support. After that he showed no sign of trying to walk by himself for weeks – and weeks – and weeks . . .

His parents became seriously worried. Edward, Tania, Andrew, and all his other contemporaries toddled about with ease. It was surprisingly painful to see other babies secure on their feet, while Lee seemed hardly to be trying.

After four more long months, Lee, now almost one and a half years old, finally managed to walk – or at least stagger. After that, of course, he didn't look back. He was soon as fast on his feet as any of his friends.

# CLIMBING, RUNNING, BALANCING

*Stairs did not pose a great problem, especially as their neighbour had three carpeted steps that were perfect for practice. (One peaceful afternoon, in his eagerness to master this skill, Lee went up and down the steps twenty-three times!)*

*After this, his passion for climbing developed apace. Success in the playground meant that the household steps had immediately to be hidden away.*

*Balance was the key to most of the new physical skills that Lee had next to achieve.*

*The timespan between learning to walk and being able to run properly was fifteen months: gradual acceleration came as Lee was able to balance better, to lift his feet higher.*

*Momentarily putting his weight on one leg in order to kick a ball seemed tricky enough, but it was far, far harder to find the co-ordination to release a ball at the right moment, and to throw it in the desired direction.*

*Lee was given a tricycle on his second birthday, but for many months he continued to push himself along with his feet on the ground on either side: pedalling was a much more advanced movement.*

# CHAIR PROBLEMS

*Skills that we all take for granted demand both patience and perseverance from the beginner. Who appreciates now what an extraordinary act of balance and aim we achieve each time we sit down backwards on to a chair?*

# DIFFICULT BEGINNINGS

During pregnancy, it's easy to get carried away imagining the instant joys of parenthood, and to forget that your tiny, frail infant may take some time to adjust to her new surroundings, particularly as regards sleeping and absorbing food.

Of course, many do settle down reasonably quickly, but at least a quarter of all new-borns experience slight or serious jaundice, especially those born early. This condition is primarily caused by the immaturity of the liver. Often the symptomatic yellowness will clear on its own but, if necessary, the baby, with her eyes covered and her skin exposed, will be treated by phototherapy. She will be placed under an ultra-violet light which will speed her full recovery.

Although jaundice is common, it is normal for mothers (even of second, third or later babies) to become temporarily uncontrollably depressed. This is partly because the jaundiced baby, like someone with a liverish hangover, is unresponsive and has no appetite; but also the protective bandages shut off the natural eye-to-eye contact which is an instinctive part of mother-baby bonding. Postnatal depression is par for the course anyway for many women as a result of hormone imbalance after labour, and it is understandable how a sad, floppy-looking infant with primrose eyes and tomato- or semolina-coloured skin may be the final factor in setting off an attack of maternal 'baby blues'.

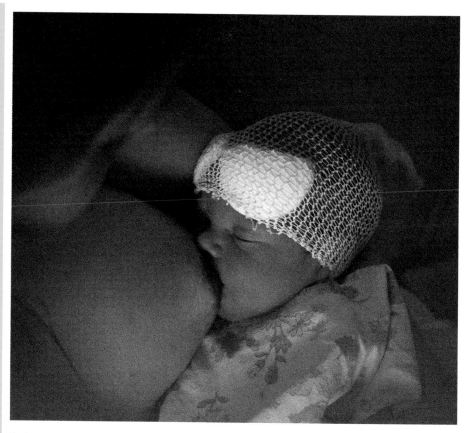

*Lee's parents had been looking forward to life as a threesome, and no one had warned them how long it might take for their new baby to establish himself into a steady pattern of eating, sleeping and generally thriving.*

*Lee, like so many otherwise healthy babies, developed jaundice on his third day. His early enthusiasm for food dwindled to nothing. For a week or more, he remained listless, unresponsive to his mother's touch.*

*If he looked yellow-orange, she felt despondently blue – a failure as a mother. Her nature seemed to change. She became silent, only breaking out of her gloom uncharacteristically to snap at her husband when he tried to cheer her. Reacting like so many new fathers whose wives suffer from postnatal depression, he suddenly saw Lee as an intruder who was ruckling their contentment as a pair.*

*When at last Lee returned to normal colouring, he began to perk up and regain the ounces he had lost in his first week. Once he was back to his birthweight, six and a half pounds, it was time to leave hospital.*

*Home together, problems forgotten; it was a wonderful moment, settling him at last into the carefully prepared cot.*

# FINDING A RHYTHM

New-born babies vary widely in their needs and demands. Gradually, as your baby's digestive system matures, she will settle into a routine, content with feeds three or four hours apart, and eventually she will sleep through the night. Some babies become comfortably established much quicker than others, even within one family. It's partly luck, partly a relaxed attitude, and partly just a matter of time.

If in any doubt, visit your local baby clinic and lean on expert advice. Regular visits are important, especially for checks on your baby's hearing as well as general health and weight gains.

*Lee started out as a night-waker and a day-sleeper. He lay so still some afternoons that his mother found herself rousing him to make sure he was still alive!*

*The nights were shattering. Feeds quietened him temporarily, but often he would start wailing again after a couple of hours. His mother panicked about whether she had enough milk, whether she ought to feed him each time he cried or just leave him yelling in the hope he would settle on his own. His father wanted to be supportive, but worried about coping at work on so little sleep.*

*If life with Lee was bewildering for his parents, it must have been even more confusing for him. He would wake, completely overwhelmed by hunger. His brain was still too immature to conjure up memories: he was living precisely in each moment, with no future and no past, so he could not reassure himself by imagining his mother, the blissful rhythm of sucking, or the comfort of a full stomach. His distress signal of crying was activated by pain and aloneness rather than by calculation to get help to his side.*

*No tears – but the most desolate sound in the world . . .*

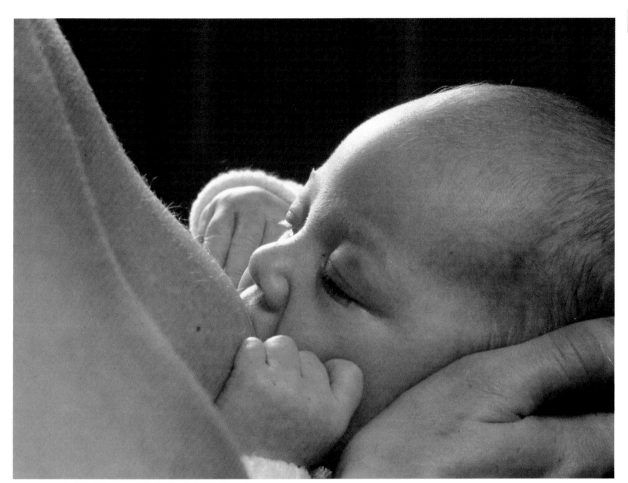

*His mother learnt that it was better for him, and thus, in the long run, better for her, if she went to him quickly. If left crying, he became so wracked by sobs that when at last she did start to feed him, he could no longer suck, only gasp in air which left him even more hungry and frustrated.*

*If she came in time, however, her soothing voice, her enveloping, gentle arms, and her milky smell made him pause in his yells. A touch on his cheek would activate his sucking reflex, and everything would become right for him as the warm liquid flowed comfortingly into his empty stomach, and his brain and body absorbed the sensations of being safe and loved.*

# INSTINCTIVE UNDERSTANDING

You may have felt an absolute bond with your baby from the moment of birth, but this state of mutual harmony might take some time to grow. A relaxed attitude often plays a part in speeding the process. The realization that you are at last succeeding in understanding and fulfilling your baby's needs, that you can communicate and be at one with her, sometimes is the most delectable experience, especially for a first-time mother. For those with a less romantic attitude, it's a great relief to sense that life is coming back under control.

A generation or two ago, people used to worry that they might 'spoil' their babies if they always picked them up when they cried.

Now research has shown that, in the first year or so, your baby's brain will not be developed enough either to recall your image when you're away from her side, or to calculate that if she cries, you'll come.

When she's just grumbling, she may drift off to sleep. When she's really wailing, it means she's uncomfortable, lonely, even afraid, and it's cruel not to go to her. There's plenty of time to be 'firm' with her when she's confident, established and able to understand the significance of what you're saying.

*As Lee's mother became keyed into his needs, at last she felt she was some use as a parent, and suddenly she experienced such a burst of tender protectiveness that tears started to well in her own eyes. She realized how disappointed she had been in the first two or three weeks, because she had assumed she would instantly bond with Lee from birth; but she had only experienced a curious blankness, peppered with occasional patches of panic as she worried whether she was capable of looking after him. Now she could admit her private disappointment at the clumsiness of her first stumbling efforts to satisfy the tiny, demanding stranger. And he wasn't a stranger any more – he was uniquely and wonderfully a part of her.*

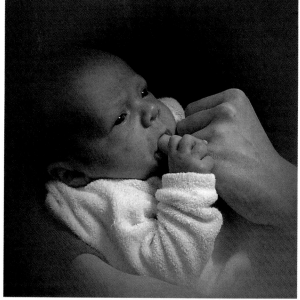

*She couldn't bear to hear him crying, but gradually came to understand whether or not it was urgent to go to him. She found she could tell by the different timbre of his wailing whether he was frantically hungry, in real discomfort, desperate or just grumbling.*

*His crying was by no means always connected with hunger. Sometimes he could be comforted by other means.*

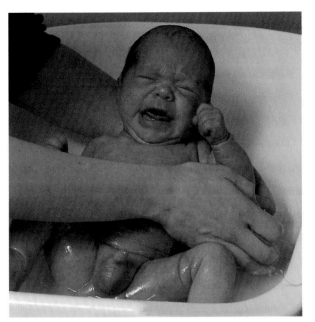

*He hated his bath, so most days his mother just sponged him over and gave him an extra-careful top and tailing.*

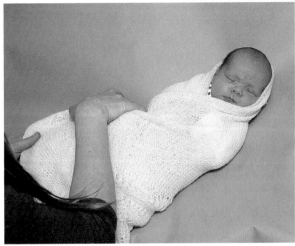

*She noticed (before he developed any muscle-tone in his body) that he was discomforted when his arms and legs were free. Even clothed, he seemed to feel insecure; he seemed relieved to be closely swaddled.*

*Swaddling was, of course, only a substitute for being cuddled. Lee's father said the baby needed love just as much as he did food.*

# BABY POWER

You might imagine that your new baby will be totally confused by the huge variety of new sights and sounds around her, but she is born with the skill to select and she is instinctively drawn to the human voice and the human face.

This is not only nature's way of helping her learn to recognize her own parents, but researchers say it also has the effect of increasing her parents' attachment to her.

She will know you by your voice before she recognizes your face. The more she reacts when you speak, the more you will find yourself wanting to talk to her; in this way, she has an inborn power to evoke the response that she needs from you.

*Lee enjoyed being talked to almost more than anything else. When his parents took turns to speak to him, he would track their voices from one to the other, turning first his ears, then his eyes – even at two weeks, which is earlier than most babies.*

*Because he responded to their voices they found themselves all the more eager to talk to him.*

*His mother discovered that she could actually stop him crying by humming or muttering in his ear, though he'd start again if she became silent. She was amazed that the sound of speech meant so much to him, long before he could possibly distinguish one word from another.*

*She was also intrigued by the way he seemed to scan her features: her hairline then her chin, the sides of her face, her mouth, nose then eyes: he was pre-programmed to learn the features of his caretaker. Equally instinctively, she found herself putting her face close enough for him to focus on.*

*As human babies are more helpless than other new-born creatures, it was another month before Lee could pick out his mother by sight, though he knew her sooner by voice and by smell. Meanwhile, he did not have any concept that he was a separate being from her, that he was a person at all. He simply felt complete when she was there.*

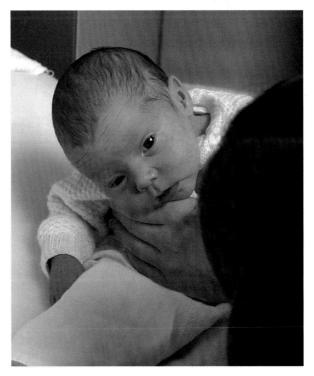

# LATE SMILER

The hardest human heart is melted by a baby's toothless smile which elicits, even from strangers, unknown depths of protective feelings: another of nature's ways of ensuring the safety of the helpless human young.

Every parent longs for the first glimpse of the baby's first real, responsive smile. However, like all landmarks in her development, the average age, six weeks, is only a rough guide. Your baby may smile back at you almost from birth or not until she is ten or even eleven weeks old.

Some parents may become over-anxious at such a delay, just as they may become over-proud if their baby appears to be otherwise ahead. Like any other developmental milepost, your baby will smile only when she is ready. Meanwhile, babies are sensitive to their parents' moods: if you worry, you may convey your tension to her, and accidentally slow the process down further.

Because smiling is a 'response', almost a reflection from your own eyes and mouth, it is important not to let your smiles switch on and off like a light, but to grin and let your eyes twinkle steadily and encouragingly, giving your baby time to react. If you stop smiling and start chattering too quickly, you confuse her and she may actually end up crying. Everything with small babies needs to be slow and gentle.

*Lee was a rather sleepy baby owing to his difficult start, and was slightly later than average in reaching several stages of development, especially in starting to smile.*

*Almost from birth, he smiled perfectly well in his sleep; some people said it was just wind, others that he was unconsciously practising for the real smile. His parents were convinced that all his expressions reflected to some extent what he felt: when he cried he looked miserable, so when he smiled, even with closed eyes, it must mean that he was contented and at peace with his new world.*

*Edward, born on the same day and in the same hospital as Lee, grinned enchantingly, reflecting his mother's smile at only five weeks.*

*Lee, always taking his own pace, remained sombrely serious for a few weeks more. He showed his appreciation of his mother's company with adorable gurgling sounds, but she wanted to see him smile. Fearing that he was backward, that something was dreadfully wrong with him, she became unnecessarily fraught.*

In due course, when he was ready, at about nine weeks, his eyes began to twinkle. Were the corners of his mouth turning up?

When his first full smile dawned, it was as if the sun had come out.

At ten weeks, he seemed to be smiling all the time, and not just at his parents – he even returned his face-splitting grin to the cheerful poster in the electricity shop!

# CHOOSING JUST ONE SPECIAL PERSON

At some point in the first four months, a baby usually attaches herself to just one special person, whom she will love and rely on most strongly throughout her first year. Normally this will be whoever spends most time with her: father, mother, grandparent or hired help (the baby cannot know who is a blood relation). Such an attachment depends not so much on efficient physical care as on the quality of love, of play and of happy times spent together.

This one-to-one loving relationship is a foundation vital to your baby's development, enabling her later to cope confidently with learning, independence and future friendships. It does not exclude her from loving other people she knows well. With any luck, your baby will not only have both parents close to her but will also have regularly attendant grandparents, neighbours or friends to enrich her experience of people and play. This will be a tremendous help when, towards the end of her first year, she goes through the stage of fearing strangers.

Sometimes, a baby in her second year may switch her favours and, temporarily at least, may seem to prefer the breadwinner of the family, the person perhaps who comes in from work with nothing else to do other than play, in contrast to the daytime caretaker who may still be drudging through endless routine. This can seem painfully unfair, but may eventually prove advantageous, especially where a new baby appears and requires a lot of her mother's attention.

*At first Lee could not tell one person from another. He knew when a comfortable pair of arms held him firmly and lovingly, but his rooting reflex sometimes led him to shock and disappointment.*

*As his awareness of taste and smell was more acute than his other senses, he soon came to know his mother as the source of his food, and probably recognized her by her voice quite early on. Once he began to smile, he bestowed his favours equally on his mother, father or anyone else who grinned at him, even, for that matter, on a paper mask of a face! By three and a half months, however, his broadest smiles were for his parents.*

*As his mother was at home with him all the time, he naturally grew closer to her. With her early depression in the past, she had now settled quite contentedly into motherhood, though sometimes of course she missed the mental activity of work and the companionship of colleagues.*

*They were so much a part of each other, he literally didn't know whether he was sucking his thumb or hers.*

She had expected the days at home to pass slowly, but her time was very full, even though Lee still slept for several hours in the afternoon. When awake, he not only needed feeding and changing but, as the months passed, he became more and more companionable, and was irresistibly responsive when entertained.

Lee's father was late home most evenings and his work often took him abroad. Whenever possible, especially at weekends, he bathed Lee and played with him. Sometimes, the mother-baby closeness made him feel rather an outsider, but Lee soon started to really recognize him even after a week's absence, and would reward his attentions with special wide smiles and chuckles. In fact his father was better at stopping him crying than his mother, especially when a feed was due.

# SELF-DISCOVERY

*At three and four months, Lee treated his mother as an extension of himself: he would suck her hair or her chin as readily as his own fist . . .*

*'This is me; this is my chin!' she would say to him.*

*He was still too young to understand that he was a separate, individual person. His mother found this idea hard to imagine, until someone pointed out that he couldn't see where he started or finished, neither the top of his head nor his toes, because he couldn't lift his head very high. He could only absorb what went on in front of his eyes, therefore his mother's face was more familiar than his own extremities.*

*She decided to help him discover the difference between him and her . . .*

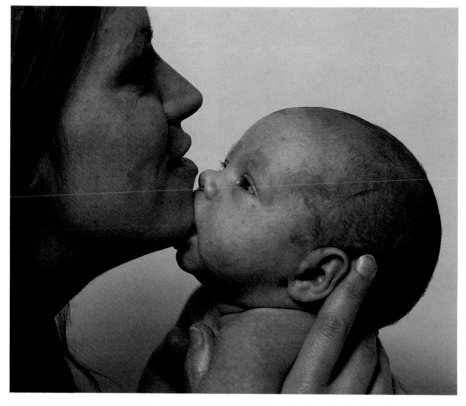

*For weeks more, when his fingers appeared in his line of vision, he didn't realize they were part of himself. To him they looked like interesting mobile objects, and he would stare at them for ages, instinctively twisting them into different shapes.*

*His toes, too, were objects of fascination, to be tasted and tested, like any other object that found its way into his grip.*

*Gradually he learnt that he could bring his hands and feet in front of his eyes on purpose. Meanwhile, his feet played with his feet and his hands with his hands, and it was a long time before he fully understood that they were his own and under his control.*

# MIRROR RESPONSES

*To help Lee's self-discovery further, his mother often held him up in front of a mirror. At three and four months, he showed no particular interest or recognition. However, at around five months, though still not interested in his own reflection, he seemed aware that the other image he saw was that of his mother.*

*It was not until around six months that he appeared to recognize himself, though even then he could just have been smiling socially at what seemed to him to be another friendly baby.*

*At eight or nine months he was utterly absorbed in the study of his own face; this was a major step towards full understanding of himself as a separate person from his mother. For many months more, he would look in his toy mirror, learning his own face and puzzling over his hands.*

*Meanwhile the possibilities for confusion were endless . . .*

# OUT OF SIGHT, OUT OF MIND

*At around the time that Lee was beginning to develop a concept of his own separate self, his memory also began to function more maturely. Previously he had simply forgotten any object that fell off his tray, but from about six months, he followed its trajectory, or looked for it after it had fallen.*

*Games like peep-bo not only amused him, but, because his mother popped so quickly in and out of sight, he could also begin to comprehend that she still existed when he couldn't see her . . .*

*Yet at around seven months, even when he watched his mother hiding his favourite truck, he still could not retain its image in his mind for the minute or so he needed for its rediscovery. He could only find it if she left a small edge sticking out . . .*

*At eight months, if he saw the toy being hidden, he would go after it and would find it every time – provided his mother used the same hiding place. But if she hid it elsewhere, even if his eyes were on her, he would be unable to adjust, and would return in vain to the first hiding place, because for him the object still only 'existed' where he had found it the first time.*

*Over the next few months he finally reached the point where he could conjure up an image of an object without seeing it; he could even understand that it had an existence independent of his, so that it could have been moved without his watching.*

# SEPARATION ANXIETY

Your baby's attachment to you grows stronger and stronger until she reaches a state of mind in which she cannot tolerate your absence for a moment. This anxiety may also be connected with her dawning awareness that you have a life of your own which goes on out of her sight. A difficult stage, instinctive rather than logical, it just has to be lived through and carefully managed so that she will not remain clingy and insecure for the rest of her life. With luck and care it will all be over within two or three months, though there may be slight lapses from time to time, especially in moments of ill health.

When you *have* to go out or leave her with a friend, it's best to play it straight, giving her a hug and kiss and a clear wave goodbye (all to the good if she can manage to wave 'bye-bye' in return). A 'ritual' like this will help her to recognize and accept what's going to happen. If you sometimes slip away on the quiet, she'll never know when you're going to do it again, and will become even more clingy. It's agony if you do have to turn your back to the sound of screams, but she'll probably settle down calmly with another safe and known adult once you are out of sight, and will only really start to fuss again on your return.

*At nine months, Lee suddenly became clingy. He couldn't bear his mother to be out of sight for an instant: she couldn't even briefly go to the bathroom without him collapsing in tears. He could no longer be decoyed into enjoying a toy for more than thirty seconds.*

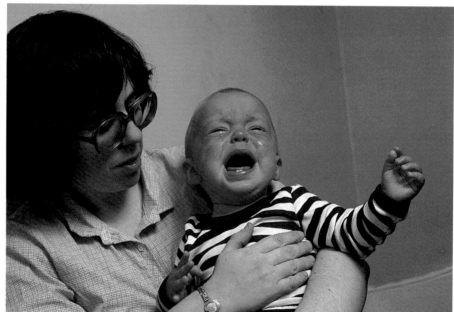

*As his fear of separation grew, of course it became harder to leave him to play at Edward's home, where he'd always been extremely happy. Once he saw that his mother was about to leave he started shrieking.*

*Gradually he could be reassured, after she had gone, but then sometimes when she returned he would cry heart-rendingly and make her feel a brute.*

*Edward reached the same stage at the same time.*

# STRANGER ANXIETY AND COMFORT HABITS

'Stranger anxiety' is related to but different from 'separation anxiety'. It can best be compared to the self-protective reaction of lambs or calves who shy away from any strange creature. Your baby will be most unusual if she doesn't go through this stage. Until eight months she will probably smile broadly for almost anyone, but suddenly you'll see her stare with icy disdain at anyone unfamiliar, particularly if they smile or try to make her laugh. At nine or ten months, she will probably hide her head in your clothes or scream blue murder if someone comes close.

It's important to respect these genuine new anxieties, which, though temporarily awkward to live with, represent a big step forward in your baby's ability to sort out who is who.

Try to encourage newcomers to stand back and let your baby get used to their presence in the room before they come in close.

Some babies suck their thumbs and twiddle their hair or ears for comfort, others have a particular cuddly toy or even a favourite bit of old blanket which may become revoltingly grubby. However, since these comfort objects live up to their title and bring visible relief and calm to a sensitive baby or toddler, it's worth putting up with them. It's useless to swap a beautiful new teddy for the beloved outworn model; with rags or blankets sometimes a clean copy can be substituted, as long as it's not so sweet and soapy smelling that the exchange is noticed.

*If familiar adults now found themselves looked at by Lee with suspicion, strangers and irregular visitors caused him real alarm. Any friendly advance was repulsed by a hostile stare. Lee actually flinched in disgust from the aunt at whom he'd smiled so enchantingly only a month before. And when she tried to take him on her lap he showered her with indignant tears . . .*

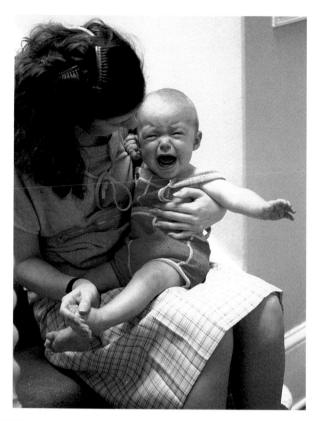

*In moments of such stress, Lee wanted to cling tightly to his mother. If she was out of reach he sucked his fingers and twiddled his ear, his 'comfort habit' – his substitute for physical contact with her. In the same way, he symbolically held on to her when settling down to sleep.*

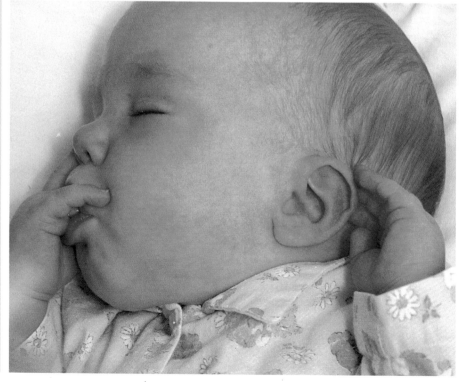

*This habit stuck with him until he was three or more. Even when his mother was right by his side, in moments of tiredness or tension in went the fingers, and his ear used to get quite red.*

# HAPPY TIMES

Apart from these minor worries, the second half of Lee's first year was particularly enjoyable for his mother. He cried much less; he was good fun; he had a wonderful sense of humour and loved to be made to laugh – and his sheer delight in her companionship was the richest of rewards. She could hardly imagine returning to her old hectic life at work. Now she could contentedly take a whole morning at Lee's pace, doing nothing more intellectual than blowing on his cheek.

She had only intended to feed him for the first month to pass on all her antibodies and to give him the best possible start. However, once she saw her friends struggling with the business of sterilizing bottles and having to heat the milk to the right temperature with a hungry baby yelling in the background, she reckoned that breast feeding was the easy way, especially if one wanted to go freely out and about. At ten months Lee was taking his milk successfully from a beaker, but she still 'topped him up' with breast milk until he was almost a year, especially at bedtime when she wanted him to settle quickly and peacefully.

Lee's father was still often late home from work, but he spent every minute he could with him. They were forever playing about and chuckling together. Lee always greeted him ecstatically, and his mother laughingly complained that she was jealous.

# FUNNY OR NAUGHTY?

To achieve maximum learning and independence, your toddler needs (supervised) freedom to explore her surroundings fully. However, not everything in the house can be suitable for her avid investigations. Though she may understand the word 'no' when she hears it, the shortness of her memory means she cannot know in advance which of her activities will upset you.

Even on her most maddening days, you will find patience and a sense of humour more effective than crossness or punishment. You are the whole core of your toddler's being. Compared with her, you are also physically huge and capable of being very frightening. A burst of anger may make you feel better but it only confuses your child who does not understand why your face has changed, why your eyes have become small and your mouth ugly as it blurts forth awful sounds.

Of course she has to learn to obey, not only for safety's sake, but also to keep daily existence tolerably civilized and to help her eventually to be able to consider others.

With your help, as her memory develops, she will anyway gradually learn what is acceptable and what is forbidden, though on the way she'll test your patience and will-power time and again. Meanwhile, whenever possible, instead of yearning for autopilot obedience, it's more constructive to encourage her natural enjoyment of co-operation. You will certainly achieve more by rewarding her with praise than by lambasting her with anger or showering her with 'Stop it!' and 'No!'.

*As Lee left behind his babyhood and became a mobile toddler, he worked his way into more and more mischief. But he wasn't being naughty on purpose. He was just following a natural and healthy desire to master and explore all that he saw.*

*His memory was still fleeting: everything was of the moment. He returned each day to twiddle the knobs of the stereo because he saw them in front of his eyes: he could not yet recall in his imagination that yesterday (and the previous day and the previous week) he had been told 'No!', 'No!' and 'No!' – though he did understand the meaning of the word and his mother's tone of voice when he heard it.*

His fascination with the lavatory was also not intentional naughtiness. Still in nappies, he had no idea of its real purpose – he saw it as a bowl with delightful, splashable water at just the right height for him. He had observed his mother only minutes before diligently cleaning it. In his eyes, the brush was her 'toy', and he was imitating her 'play'.

Even at eighteen months his memory was still short-lived – and temptation was overwhelming. Indeed he wanted her to join in his new-found game. Rebuke was useless: the only answer was to keep the bathroom door shut.

This stage was often maddening and Lee's mother caught herself getting ridiculously cross. She suddenly heard how she sounded when Lee picked up her constantly repeated 'No!' and started using it back at her. She decided that it was more effective to establish good habits than to punish Lee before he was old enough to understand. She made a game each evening of putting the bricks back in their box; and invented enjoyable shared rituals like putting the cuddly toys to bed before allowing Lee lots of splashy fun in the bath.

# 'ME DO IT'

Maintaining patience in the face of your toddler's growing independence becomes harder as she progresses through her second year. No longer a baby, she is not yet a child. Her instinct is to pull away from you, like a fledgling trying to fly from the nest, or like any other young animal prompted by nature to fend for itself. Human infants feel this urge for an uncomfortably long period before they are able to cope on their own.

As she begins to develop her own ambitions, it's important to spare extra time to allow her to pursue her ideas; otherwise, she can actually learn helplessness, and become far more reliant on assistance than is good for her – or for you.

She will want to manage everything for herself but of course she needs you there when things go wrong; once comforted, she will hurtle off to try independence again, until the next disaster, and the next. It's up and down all the time. But your toddler's face when she triumphs makes it all worthwhile.

*Lee couldn't bear to be helped, even when hunger made him too impatient to manage on his own. Mealtimes, which had been so easy until he was fifteen months, suddenly became a struggle. Having shrieked to start eating, now he refused to finish his plateful, because, his mother eventually discovered, he was growing less in his second year, and temporarily required less food.*

*He cried more frequently than in his first year, mainly out of frustration. He still fought confinement in his play-pen, yet, when left to crawl freely, he couldn't cope emotionally with the smallest obstacle.*

*If he endlessly removed his clothes, at least this was a first stage towards his longed-for achievement of being able to dress himself.*

*Of course it was quicker and easier to do things for him. But Lee's mother realized that he needed the satisfaction of building up his own independence – so, when time allowed, she waited and watched, offering him only the slightest tactful assistance if he got stuck, and boosting him with admiration and praise when he succeeded.*

# DEALING WITH TANTRUMS AND DEFIANCE

Nearly all toddlers have tantrums, often without apparent reason. It's no use punishing your child when she does; she needs your help and reassurance to find her way back into herself. You may find that the best way of coping is to take her in your arms, if possible sitting down somewhere comfortable, and hold her tightly and lovingly, while talking to her affectionately until her fury subsides. If a tantrum erupts – as all too frequently it does – when one is out shopping or somewhere public, this is still the best solution, and is much more effective than a slap or an embarrassed retreat. Most parents at some stage have experienced similar short crises, and passers-by are often surprisingly sympathetic.

And when your toddler is mischievous, even defiant, you might find yourself feeling more proud than worried. It's sad when a child does not have enough spirit to test her will against her parents.

It's all part of growing up, part of her discovery that she can influence people as well as events by her actions. (It's also part of being able to stand up to others at school and later in life.) By two and a half, if she finds she can rouse you to anger, she may take the risk just for the pleasure of feeling she can get a reaction from you.

A common-sense approach is better than strong discipline. It's important not to crush her growing individuality and high spirits, though of course, gently and seriously, you have to teach her where the boundaries lie.

*Sometimes Lee's frustrations blew up into temper tantrums. The first of these seemed to start without reason when he was only fourteen months. He was playing relaxedly with a flower, then suddenly, howling with rage, he beat it to pieces.*

Fortunately Lee did not go in for daily tantrums like some children. When he did explode, it was usually at the most embarrassing moments – the time his father's boss came to supper, for example – and at his aunt's wedding, just as the couple were exchanging vows. His mother learnt to be wary of when he was over-tired or over-excited, or when there was tension in the house. Then she tried to slow him down and divert him.

But it wasn't always possible to stop the course of his frustration and rage. The tantrums were not his fault, and certainly were not intentional; they were just a part of growing up: a prelude to gaining control over his emotions.

The next stage was not altogether easy, either. As Lee's imagination and experience grew, he was able to picture in his mind his intended mischief together with his parents' likely disapproval. Then the tantrums faded, but he began to be naughty on purpose, an important (but tiresome) next stage in the development of both his independence and his personality. A parental 'No!' suddenly became a thrilling challenge, and he was ready to put up with anger, even punishment, in order to test how far he could go. Now that he had the vocabulary to understand what was going on, it was a good time to start quietly but firmly laying down limits . . .

# USING THE POT

For the first fifteen to twenty months your baby will be unaware of either wetting or soiling. It will be obvious when she begins to notice her bowel movements – then is the moment to introduce her to the proper purpose of her pot. (Some parents wait longer, until speech is advanced enough to discuss rationally the advantage of using a pot – in which case training may work in just a few days.) Some toddlers take much longer than others to get everything under control. Any sort of pressure is counter-productive. It's best just to encourage your baby's natural desire for independence, and to help her towards the triumph she will feel in managing for herself.

*When Lee was still only thirteen months, his grandmother rather pointedly turned up with a pot. His mother knew he was too young to understand its purpose, let alone ready to control his bladder or his bowels, but she decided to see what Lee made of it, in order not to hurt her mother-in-law's feelings.*

She then put the pot to one side for several months, until Lee was obviously aware of his bowel movements. Taking a relaxed and slow approach, she wooed Lee into co-operation unusually quickly.

Soon he was not only clean and dry by day, but he could use his new word-combining skills (see p. 86) to ask for help:

'Wee-wees – poo-poo – quick!'

# BEDTIME ROUTINE

By six or eight months, it is just as well to have worked your baby into a regular bedtime routine; looking through a picture book or sharing simple rhymes and songs, with a cuddle and a kiss before she's tucked in.

However well this works for the first few months, unfortunately, sooner or later, you are likely to meet a patch of resistance. For the sake of future good habits and your peace and sanity, it's worth being firm and consistent, never allowing her to return to the living room, nor playing with her nor giving her another feed. She should be settled back into bed without any fuss; but it's worth making sure she knows you are nearby, otherwise she might develop a genuine fear of being left alone.

She may go to bed easily, but be a painfully early riser. She may remain happy in her cot for many months longer than Lee, especially if you leave a good selection of playthings (and possibly something she likes to eat) laid out for her to find in the morning. However, if she develops a claustrophobic hatred of bars, the only solution is immediately to give her more freedom. Eventually she'll learn to climb over cot railings and will need a bed anyway.

Safety is the main problem when you promote your toddler from cot to bed. No doubt you will already have checked electric plugs, windows etc. Every possible danger must be foreseen.

*Lee had always been a good sleeper, but half-way through his second year, he started to play up.*

*His mother tried every kind of tactful persuasion. She had previously always been very successful in getting him to drop off, through a nightly ritual of looking at books and singing his favourite songs until his eyes began to close.*

*Now this early routine suddenly ceased to work: he would seem to be asleep, but as soon as the door was shut he would be roaring.*

She would have to cuddle him
back to sleep in her arms – about
three times each night.

Remembering how Lee had hated
his play-pen, his mother
wondered whether he was
distressed by the bars of his cot,
and whether, with his urge for
independence, he felt unduly
restricted.

She bought a low bed with short
safety rails so he couldn't roll out
accidentally. This was an instant
success. No longer imprisoned
behind bars, Lee relaxed, and
returned to his good old sleeping
habits.

# FEARS AND PHOBIAS

In her first year, your baby may be alarmed by loud noises, bouncy animals, or probably by something else quite unpredictable. However, her reaction is spontaneous; she is still too young to be able to build up fear in her imagination.

Only in her second year, as she becomes more aware of the uncontrollability of the world about her, however secure she is, certain things may start repeatedly to worry her.

She may be overwhelmed with fright when she comes face-to-face with a neighbour's dog, and develop a phobia about all sorts of animals, or she could develop a fear of heights. Some children become terrified of the way water swirls into the plug-hole of the bath, perhaps suffering an illogical fear that they may also be sucked down.

Getting your child used to whatever distresses her, with gentle sympathy and not too much insistence, her fears will probably quickly pass. However, nothing can be rushed. For instance, if, like so many children, she's afraid of the dark, to avoid nightmares a night-lamp may be needed for months – even years.

*Towards the end of his first year, Lee developed a terror of the vacuum cleaner. Once his mother understood what was bothering him, she only used it when he was fast asleep. A couple of months later, when he heard it in a neighbour's house, he hardly noticed it.*

*He had never been frightened of cats or dogs, but when, at eighteen months, his mother thought he would be enchanted by a baby rabbit, he unexpectedly recoiled in horror. Thereafter he shrank away and wept at the sight of the neighbour's friendly old cat whom he'd known all his life. Even coming face-to-face with a furry mechanical toy was alarming.*

*His mother invented games to try to work him through his fears. Though irrational in adult eyes, to him they were painfully real and not to be taken lightly, otherwise they could become lifelong phobias.*

*At times it was difficult to foresee just what he would find frightening. His mother forgot, when urging him to brave the slide, that, though it was only waist-height against her, in his eyes the distance down was huge.*

*But she was very sympathetic when he suddenly became distressed by anything sticky. To avoid letting this become a tiresome complex, she gave him plenty of play opportunities to enable him to work through his disgust.*

# PREPARING FOR THE NEW BABY

News of 'a lovely little brother or sister to play with' is not such a thrill for the toddler as it is for the proud parents. Your first child will probably be perfectly happy as the only one and will find it difficult to understand why you want another.

A great deal of tact and gentle humour is required in preparing her for what may well seem to her an unwelcome intruder.

*Lee's mother waited until she was visibly pregnant before she told Lee the new baby was expected.*

*She thought she might build up his enthusiasm for babies by introducing him to Andrew's new sister, whom she, of course, found irresistible. Lee found little Laura uninteresting, but was perturbed by his mother's involvement.*

*Andrew's mother pointed out all the likely problems. Despite the care she had taken to forestall any jealousy, though Andrew often appeared fond of baby Laura, his hugs were tighter than seemed comfortable.*

*Lee's mother was glad that she had waited before having a second baby; at almost three Lee was old enough to talk and to understand at least some explanations about the newcomer. Though he could not be persuaded to take an interest in other people's babies, she found he was intrigued by the idea of himself when he was just born.*

*She dug out the box of old baby clothes, and showed Lee just how much he'd grown, pointing out that he would be able to help take care of his new baby.*

# FACING A RIVAL

However well you think you have prepared your child for the arrival of a new baby, it is not fair to expect a demonstration of instant love from her. An older child may be intrigued enough to want immediately to share the caring, but toddlers cannot hide their true feelings.

For your toddler's sake, it is better at first in her presence almost to ignore the baby and to make an extra fuss of her, to underpin her sense of security and to help convince her that she's not being ousted.

*Lee's grandmother came to stay when the baby was due.*

*His mother went into hospital around midnight and had a rapid and much easier labour (as usually happens with second babies); and his father was able to get home from the hospital, give Lee breakfast and tell him the news.*

*Despite all the careful preparations and explanations, Lee just didn't want to know. He wouldn't even look at his new sister.*

*Only when his mother handed the intruder to his grandmother would he agree to take so much as one peep.*

*No use yet as a companion for play – she wasn't at all interested in the toy he held out to her.*

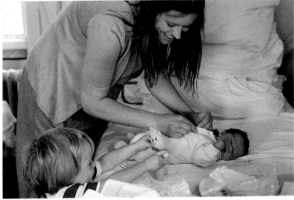

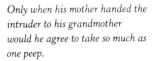

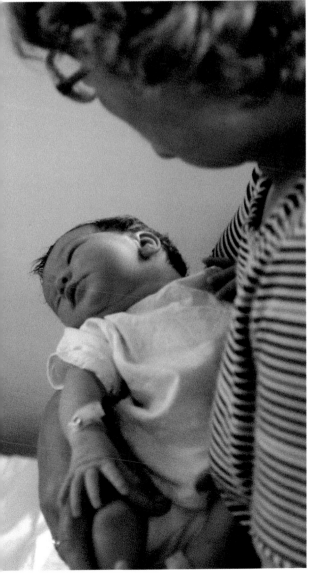

*His mother was able to come out of hospital quickly, and immediately tried to involve Lee in caring for baby Marie . . . Hold that little, wriggling thing – horrors!*

# SETTLING DOWN TOGETHER

If this period of adaptation goes amiss, jealousy can become deeply ingrained and last a lifetime; so it's crucial to be ultra-sensitive about what may seem like a real threat to your two- or three-year-old.

Though rivalry between brothers and sisters usually emerges to a greater or lesser degree, sibling friendships are also some of the best and warmest relationships that can exist, and it's worth a lot of extra effort on the part of parents to try to smooth over the natural ructions that occur throughout childhood.

*Lee's mother tried to make a game of encouraging Lee to help.*

*Despite all her efforts, he was seriously thrown, and returned to his old ear-twiddling, thumb-sucking comfort habits – with a difference.*

*. . . he started up another game of his own – attention-grabbing.*

*But gradually, as he felt less threatened and sensed that he was not in any way losing out on his parents' attention or affection, he settled down, and even tried to be helpful.*

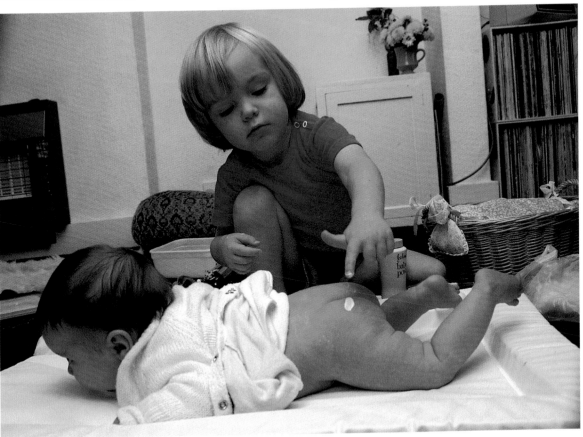

# PRE-SPEECH

*From the moment of birth, Lee seemed to appreciate being talked to by his parents. He preferred a female voice – part of his inborn mother-attachment instinct.*

*Sometimes his mother would chat away, enjoying his alert pleasure, and other times they would stare peacefully and silently for many minutes into each other's eyes. His father laughingly called these exchanges their 'conversations', and he was more right than he knew, for they were building up a pattern of communication crucial to the future development of language.*

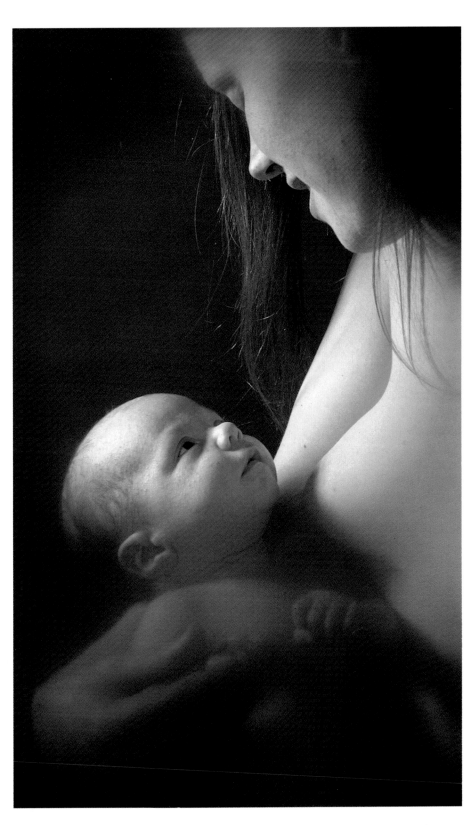

In his second month, Lee started making adorable small sounds in his throat: breathy 'Hhh-Gergergerg's. He only seemed to gurgle this way when relaxed and contented, and mostly when alone.

Eventually he developed broader vowel sounds – 'Aaagh' and 'Ooo' – which he sometimes uttered in quite long sequences. Cooing and burbling, he would look into space, as if he were practising speech noises rather than trying to communicate. But later he would sometimes appear to be having a one-way conversation with the toy at the side of his cot.

At twelve weeks he was most vocal when 'chatting' face-to-face with his mother or father, though after a while he would stop short, as if he were bored with just one admirer, and would start to address his sounds towards his other parent, or even towards the electric light or a flower-vase.

# BABY-TALK AND BODY LANGUAGE

When your baby is three or four months old, whatever your prior intentions, you may catch yourself using the most ridiculous baby language, in a peculiar treble voice, which might embarrass you in your more objective moments. But let your instinct lead you – your baby likes it.

Be aware of what's happening to your face, too – you may find your features curled into exaggerated expressions (more easily interpretable by an infant) – perhaps wide-eyed surprise with a pouting mouth, or a really crinkled frown as you express your mock dismay at a minor disaster . . .

Don't worry – you're not going mad – you are just taking natural cues from your baby: this is an important stage in the development of baby-parent communication, and you will grow out of it when she no longer needs it.

*A couple of weeks later, Lee's mother noticed that she was following his cues in speech rather than him copying her. She could hear herself speaking in an absurd, high-pitched, almost sing-song way – 'Funny little boy. Look what mummy's doing. Ironing the socks.' Lee responded excitedly to her soprano baby-talk, but if she forced herself down into her normal, low adult voice, he lost interest.*

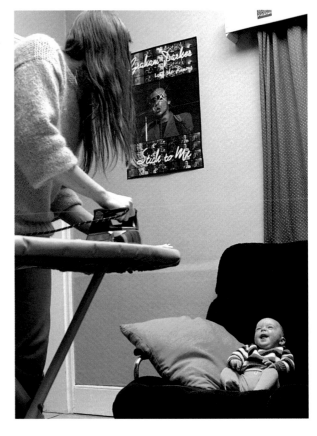

*Then she noticed that he could make her look in the direction he wanted! It was natural for her to follow his gaze to see what had attracted him when he turned his head. At four and a half months, he seemed instinctively aware that he could take her glance with his. He would look eagerly towards an object and she would bring him to it, talk about it and let him touch it.*

*At five months, without a single word, he could often make himself clearly understood just with facial expressions and body language:*

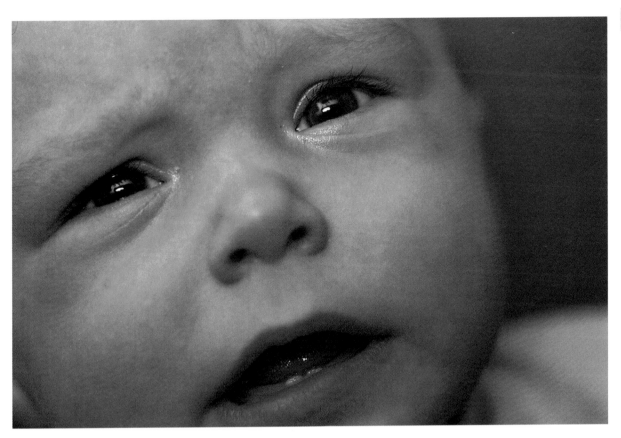

'My gums hurt.'

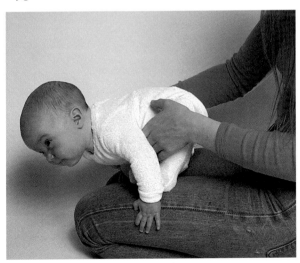

'I want to get up and go.'

'Pick me up!'

He continued to use signs and
body language long after speech
had become well-established.

# CONFIDENCE TO LOOK OUTWARD

Your baby will not be able to formulate proper words until her brain has reached the right stage of development, and the area of her mouth and throat has grown into a more mature shape. Meanwhile her future ability to communicate will be helped forward not so much by her intellect as by plenty of loving attention. She will probably talk earlier if you are always sensitive and responsive to how she is feeling, and if you amuse and stimulate her with cheerful chat and a suitable variety of things that she can observe and enjoy.

Babies reared in institutions or in difficult or over-busy homes are often slower to develop speech, not only because they receive less stimulation, but also because they are less confident. Their insecurity may make them cling and (literally) look inwards as they turn to their caretakers for reassurance. The secure baby sits unruffled in her mother's arms and stares at everything about her, building up her memory and learning all the time.

However, some clever, confident babies are also comparatively late in speaking, especially those who pour their energies into developing their physical skills: walking early, climbing stairs, engineering their toys, etc.

*Lee liked books long before he could learn words from them. He could recognize the content of clear, bright pictures, especially photographs, though he was not yet mature enough to understand that each object had its own name, neither could he yet properly separate the sound of one word from another. He chuckled at his mother because of the funny face and noises she was making when she kept on saying, 'Banana, banana, banana . . .'*

*Though it was too soon to get Lee to repeat words, his visual understanding of the pictures was a start towards acquiring speech, and his mother did her best to make them come alive.*

*Even more important was their shared delight in everything they did together. For the time being they understood each other very well without language. Enjoying this communication in the pre-speech stage meant that Lee would instinctively be all the more eager to find words when he was ready.*

# FIRST WORDS

Babies all over the world are 'programmed' in their first year to work their way through all the consonants, vowels, clicks, shushes and grunts met in every language from Australian Pygmy to Ancient Greek, Chinese, English, Hindi, Hungarian, Italian and French. Each of these sounds will emerge in varying frequency and will usually start in roughly the same order. (Deaf babies will follow the same pattern of speech development, at least for the first six months.) It is as if they are practising to be ready for whichever language they are going to hear most and grow up with. They will usually start with vowels, especially the 'a' and the 'e', which are produced in the front of the mouth; 'u' as in 'fun' and 'o' as in 'cot' may soon follow. The first consonants are likely to come from the back of the throat: a breathy 'h' or 'hg', then a 'w' or 'k', followed by 't', 'p', 'd' and 'm' sounds which are produced nearer the front of the mouth.

At some time between eight months and one year, your baby is likely to run pairs of consonants together. In many languages the words Mama, Papa and Baba have similar meanings, as these are the first word-like sounds produced by babies everywhere.

*Lee was no exception: his first utterings with recognizable meaning were 'Mama' then 'Baba'. However, these were accidental words emerging from the world-wide, inter-racial pattern of baby-babbling and had not been learnt as a result of his imitating his parents. Rather they imitated him when he uttered these double sounds by chance, and therefore reinforced them into his memory by their echoing enthusiasm.*

*His first real word was 'bo', which he learnt from his favourite game of peep-bo.*

*Meanwhile he certainly understood much more than he could say. The age-old baby games formed a very important part of learning to recognize words, and, of course, he loved them: 'Round and round the garden' made him chuckle in anticipation of being tickled.*

'Patacake' was good for co-ordination as well as for speech development. 'This little piggy' helped to give him an early feeling for numbers and counting.

It was hard to know exactly when he understood words and when he was just interpreting his mother's voice: he crawled straight to his high chair when she said, 'Tea-time!' – but was he taking his cue from the actual word, or from the tone she always used to announce meals? Or was it from the clever way he followed with his eyes the direction in which she was looking?

# GIVE A DOG A NAME

As your baby/toddler enjoys producing an effect, she will be boosted by your enthusiasm when she comes out with a new word. She will be even more encouraged when she finds that she can use words effectively to get what she wants or to obtain help when she needs it.

Some toddlers don't utter a single word until they are over two, while some start at nine or ten months. There's no hurry about learning to speak any more than there's a race to crawl or to walk. Your baby will reach each of these milestones exactly when she is ready. Your relaxed and warm approval will greatly reinforce her efforts, but any kind of pressure will have a negative effect. If she senses that you want her to say or to do something, and she cannot understand what it is, she will become flustered and unreceptive. If she's having fun, she'll pick up language (and other skills) with self-propelled enthusiasm.

However, naturally it helps if the people around her talk to her, using simple sentences, share picture books with her and help her to 'label' objects. Sometimes younger children are late in learning to speak because their older brothers and sisters instinctively comprehend what they need, and say things for them. In other families, the toddler picks up language faster because the next child up is still using few and simple sentences. Sometimes a baby is so busy concentrating on her physical development, she doesn't have time for speech. Each individual child is different and there is no exact timetable.

At twelve months, Lee understood quite a lot, but only spoke five words: 'Mama', 'Dada', 'bo', 'bye-bye' and 'er-ger' (his own word for 'Give me!'). His sixth word later became 'dat' (that), which he used when pointing.

At last he looked straight at the neighbour's labrador and said, 'Dog.'

His parents were just celebrating his accuracy when he went to hug the cat, looked proudly towards them and again said, 'Dog.'

Even the bauble on the Christmas tree was 'dog' for a while . . .

In fact using the wrong word represented greater progress than they realized: it meant that he'd discovered that words were for naming objects or people.

*Now his vocabulary grew slowly but steadily, at first by only three or four words a month. Labelling things became a good game.*

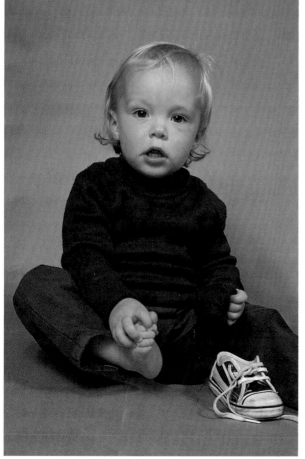

*Sometimes he would suddenly produce a new word in a moment of drastic need: frustrated by failure to get the shoes on to his feet, and desperate to attract his mother's attention, he suddenly cried out, 'Shoozh!'*

# VISUAL AND VERBAL CONNECTIONS

Up to about thirteen or fourteen months, your toddler can only make a connection between two objects by physical means: banging her plate on the table; squashing the ring of keys into her beaker; using a spoon to get food into her mouth.

It is a most important step in her development when she starts to recognize *in her mind* the relationship of one object to another: when she can conceive that the key belongs to the door and the brush to the dust-pan, and understands that such connections exist without her doing anything about them. This is the beginning of being able to think about things happening rather than physically making them happen.

The next stage, which is crucial to the development of speech, is when she begins to be able to symbolize an object or action in her mind with a word rather than a picture.

*Soon Lee began to use voice inflexion to convey the different meanings of a single word. For example, when he said 'Dink', his mother could tell whether he was demanding a drink, asking where he could find his mug or just passing comment as the mug caught his eye.*

*For some time, he still could only use one word at a time. However, he was starting to be able to associate two ideas in his mind. He used this new skill to get round the difficulty of his lack of vocabulary. He didn't know the word for shirt, but he knew who wore one: 'Dada'.*

'Mama'                    'Man'

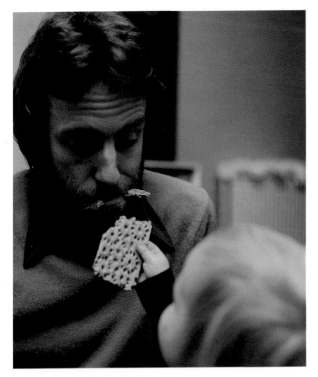

Sometimes he would use a phrase run into one word, like 'Eaty-tup!' or 'Whazzat?' But it was some months more before he reached the point where he was able to put two words together. He needed to be able both to visualize a biscuit and to imagine putting it into his mouth; then at last he could put this happy thought into words, and come out with his first true sentence: 'Eaty-tup bicket!'

A sentence consisting of three words, 'Me go stairs', followed quite soon, but 'Dada eaty-tup bicket!' took months more, because it involved the complicated process of being able to imagine his father eating rather than himself.

With adjectives, he had to widen his understanding by experience. He learnt the difference between 'good' and 'bad' by his mother's tone of voice long before the actual word became clear to him. For safety's sake, she made sure that he understood that 'hot' was painful, then she made an enjoyable game playing with ice to help him discover the meaning of 'cold'.

# NATURAL GRAMMAR AND UNDERSTANDING

Your toddler's language development is stimulated by her increasing recognition and understanding of everything around her. Toys and books help, but are not enough on their own. She also needs occasional new sights and new experiences – seeing animals in the country perhaps, or visiting a duck-pond or a garage. Meanwhile, by her absorbing what you say to her and hearing adult conversation going on over her head, her speech grows naturally.

It is more important to chatter cheerfully with her than to consciously teach or insist on correct sentences. These will emerge anyway in good time, but meanwhile she'll learn most successfully through the stimulus of play and the triumph of being able to communicate effectively in her own short-forms.

*Lee's comprehension remained more advanced than his speaking vocabulary. By the time he was two, he could follow quite complicated instructions about picking up leaves, putting them into a lorry, pushing them along and tipping them out again at a certain point.*

*However, when the autumn chill got to him and he found himself in real distress, he reverted to body language rather than words to express his discomfort.*

As his speech grew, he seemed to pick up a basic grammar by ear. At around two and a half, he came out with several accurate and innaccurate, but always logical, versions of the past tense: 'Lee washed face', '...goed shop', '...see'd pussy'. He could also form plurals: 'housez' – and, of course, 'mousez' instead of 'mice'. Without being taught, he used (in a moment of fury) a possessive pronoun: 'My car!' to his friend Tania, followed by an equally emphatic and correct accusative: 'Gi' me!'

A few weeks later, he said 'Naughty Tarny' when Tania grabbed a chair, and 'Tarny naughty' when his mother came to see what was bothering him. His grammar was his own selective version, and he was not yet ready or willing to be taught a full or correct sentence by his parents. It didn't matter. There was plenty of time for his brain to mature enough to cope with longer sentences, and meanwhile it was a joy to experience his growing triumphs of communication.

# BEFORE HANDS

*Staring was Lee's first form of play. Every day his parents would take him sightseeing around the room, bringing all sorts of objects within his range of focus of seven to fourteen inches. He was too unco-ordinated to reach out and touch, but his eye was selective: his glance was irresistibly drawn towards patches of light or shiny reflections. He liked bright colours, especially red, and he was particularly enthralled by the black and white squares of the chess-board.*

*However, his father's face was still the most interesting pattern.*

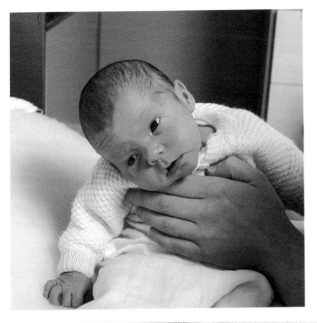

Of course he didn't need to be busy looking at things all his waking hours. Indeed he spent long periods dreamily gazing at nothingness. His mother called these quiet moments his 'inner growing'.

His hearing was better developed than his sight. Human voices and music were his favourite sounds. He would cry at any sudden or loud noise. Being a slightly nervous baby, he was startled and distressed even by a small rattle; he was not yet able to get his hand around it comfortably or make it sound without help.

His fist was still bunched-up tight. He couldn't even separate a finger to munch on, let alone handle toys in the conventional sense.

It was a matter of weeks (longer than with most babies) before he could separate the fingers enough to stuff them comfortingly into his mouth.

# EASILY BORED

From the very first weeks, your baby needs plenty of different things to look at.

While she stares about her and (literally) sizes up all that she sees, her brain is building up a remarkable geometrical understanding of proportion, shape and distance. She is thus able to recognize familiar forms, even though she cannot remember them when they are out of her sight.

At about four months, her sight and focus are almost the same as those of an adult. Her judgement of distance and size is remarkably advanced compared with the other workings of her brain: for instance, she will spread her arms wide for a balloon, but keep her hands cupped for a small brick.

*Though Lee could not remember anything unless it was right in front of his eyes, he could recognize familiar shapes as soon as he saw them, and, even before he was a month old, was already stimulated by variety and bored by repetition.*

*Linear patterns particularly attracted his attention, perhaps because hard, clear lines made more sense to his hazy vision than soft curves or pastel colours. He soon graduated from the chess-board, which had first appealed to him, preferring increasingly complicated layouts like the multi-coloured check of his father's shirt.*

*Slight variations in objects attracted him more than anything totally new: the framed photo he stared at enthralled for ten minutes one day was less compelling the next; but when his mother showed him a similarly-shaped shiny mirror, again he became alert, studious and intent.*

*The same would apply to bricks: yesterday's were only briefly interesting, but just a slight variation – red instead of blue, shiny plastic instead of wooden – and he would switch on his stare, learning thoroughly each new facet.*

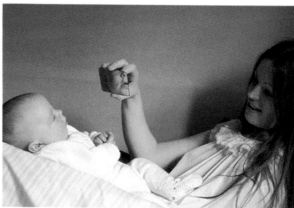

*Only at around three months did he start to appreciate more complicated shapes, like soft toys, plastic ducks – or those intriguing wiggly pink objects that he did not yet know as his own toes.*

*At four months, he could focus further away from his eyes. Anything new to look at filled him with happiness. The flicker of the sun-lit, breeze-blown blossom made him wriggle, kick and chortle with delight . . .*

*. . . though he would bawl with boredom if faced yet again with the same old set of pram-beads.*

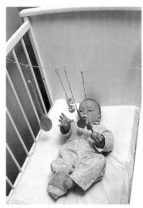

*Taking utmost care to keep any string safely away from Lee's neck, his mother made her own collection of play oddments, looking around the house for something to add each day. Lee always went straight to the newest item.*

# TESTING AND TASTING

Discovery is a very important part of play.

Your baby's inner lips and tongue are more sensitive at this stage than her fingertips, so she will instinctively bring everything that comes her way to her mouth. She is testing texture rather than taste.

(Take care to keep all medicines, household bleaches and other poisons out of reach. For some reason, unpleasant smells do not deter small children from their explorations, and accidents through poisoning are frighteningly frequent.)

*For Lee, even the simplest household objects were new and, therefore, exciting. As his hands became more competent, he grabbed and explored whatever came his way. For him, everything was a toy, insomuch as he felt an unquenchable urge to discover both what it looked like and how it felt.*

*His friend Edward had a dummy, but Lee's mother preferred her son to do without, even if it meant putting up with slightly more crying, to give him every possible chance for his new discoveries.*

*As Lee put everything he could grab straight to his mouth, his introduction to solid food was accidental – more like play than any organized or intentional decision to supplement his diet. In the relaxed atmosphere of a family gathering, his mother didn't know whether to feel guilty or amused that his first ecstatic experience of solid food was chocolate – part of an Easter egg. After that he wanted to try some of everything she ate . . .*

*To keep Lee interested in his exploration and enjoyment of eating, his mother gave him different tastes and textures to try. At this stage, he didn't really need any supplement to breast milk and the amount he actually ate was minimal, but it was a good way to introduce foods containing essential vitamins and minerals as well as to prevent future faddiness. Sometimes new flavours took some getting used to, but Lee's curiosity and enthusiasm made him persist.*

# WEANING THROUGH PLAY

It is not strictly conventional to look upon even the most cheerful weaning as play, but such an attitude will make this stage much easier.

Of course weaning can also be a worrying business, and some parents become obsessive about whether their baby is getting enough or the right food. An adequate and varied diet is certainly vital, and advice from experts at the local clinic important. But when it comes to actually getting the food down your baby's throat, a relaxed and playful atmosphere at feed time is likely to be far more successful than a tense or determined approach.

Eating is, after all, one of the greatest pleasures in life.

*Tasting things was fun and the spoon was, in Lee's eyes, just another toy, for grabbing, exploring and mastering. Soon he was managing to get at least an adequate fraction of each meal into his mouth. Even at five months, he still hardly needed cereal: indeed too much would make him fat, so it didn't matter that most went overboard. The mess was never unbearable as his bib caught any spillage.*

*By the time he had grown enough to need more, he was becoming more efficient with the spoon. Sometimes his mother was in a hurry, or was anxious that he wasn't getting enough. So as not to hurt his pride, she still let him feed himself, but had a second spoon to hand which she tactfully darted to his mouth while he was absorbed in the play-skill of picking up cereal.*

*Food as a pleasure and eating as a game, had given him a great advantage over his contemporaries, who were still behaving like sparrows – opening their mouths wide and waiting for food and drink to be popped in.*

*Of course not everything could go smoothly. Lee gave his mother a hard time about learning to use a mug. Her presence reminded him that there was another perfectly good way of drinking . . .*
*His father was therefore far more successful in helping him develop his skill with the teacher-beaker.*

# PARENT PLAY

*Almost everything Lee did beyond breathing, digesting and sleeping was play. He was playing not only when he explored new food or mastered his spoon, but also when he listened to new sounds, splashed in his bath, explored the hinges of his books, or struggled to climb the stairs.*

*Above all else he liked playing with his parents. His mother's hair or face or hands were more mobile and much better to play with than any man-made toy.*

*Through physical play, he received his earliest preparation for sport: learning about speed, courage and excitement. Being rather nervous, he wasn't happy at first as his father swooped him up in his arms . . .*

*. . . but with gentle encouragement, his reaction to horseplay became more robust.*

*His parents were not only good toys but also an excellent means of transport before he could crawl.*

*They provided ideal furniture on which he could practise pulling himself up . . .*

*. . . and the perfect cradle.*

# DEVELOPING HAND-SKILLS

*Through play, Lee became more and more skilful with his hands.*

*For the first three or four months, his hand was little more than a sort of grasping clamp on the end of his straight forearm; he couldn't flex his wrist or use his fingers and thumb separately.*

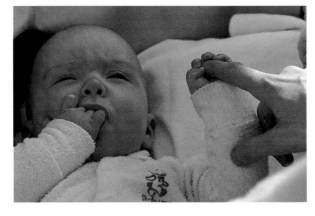

*Once his co-ordination of hand and eye improved, and he progressed from swiping out at what he saw to reaching for it in a more organized manner, his wrists were still straight, his full-fisted grasp clumsy, even when he was involved in eating his first book.*

*As he played, exploring all sorts of different toys and household objects, his wrist-joints gradually became more supple, until he could delicately stroke and feel, examine textures, differentiate between soft and hard, smooth and rough.*

*For a long time, he couldn't use his finger in opposition to his thumb, and even picked daisies with a circular grasp.*

*At around ten months, he was beginning awkwardly to bring his thumb and finger together.*

*At eleven months, he had developed a fine pincer movement that enabled him to pick up even the tiniest objects.*

Play
# LETTING GO

Releasing an object on purpose is neurophysically much more advanced than picking it up – when you see your baby apparently gripping a prized small trophy, she may soon start howling with frustration because she cannot let it go. This sometimes seems incredible, especially with those sporting babies who delight in the larger movements of chucking things about or knocking plates of food off the trays of their high chairs.

Your baby may enjoy a game of trying to hand slightly larger objects to and fro between you, and, if carried out with humour and much patience, it should help her overcome this otherwise tiresome limitation on her activities.

This awkwardness in letting go can continue to be a nuisance to your baby perhaps even up to eighteen months, and may cause her difficulties in building brick towers or in carrying out other such actions that she will instinctively attempt.

*From his earliest days, though Lee grasped anything that touched his palm, he could not let go, even when his exhaustion from holding made him cry with discomfort.*

*Though at nine months he could quite skilfully manipulate with one or two hands, he could not relax his grip at will, though he would passively let go when his fist became tired.*

*Even when his pincer grip was impressively precise, he could still not voluntarily release anything small. At eleven months, when his mother urgently wanted him to give her the hot chilli before he put it to his mouth, though he touched her outstretched palm and used both hands in his effort to get rid of it, he could not relax his hold, so that eventually she had to uncurl his fingers and take it from him.*

*Months later, he was still using two hands to let go.*

# EXPLORATION AND DISCOVERY

The amount a baby incidentally learns as she goes about her daily play is fascinating. She wants to find out by touch how everything works; she may be as interested in the hinges of her board book as in the pictures. Soap is slippery when wet, her father's sweater is scratchy, the pile of the carpet is curious and brush-like to her endlessly probing fingers. No baby is born knowing that a saucepan is curved and heavy, and that her plastic cup fits inside it. She needs to find out in her own way, in her own time. Everything she discovers will be accumulated later into useful general knowledge, a necessary basis for her future formal education, and she should always be encouraged in her 'research'.

Sometimes, however, too much emphasis can be placed on the importance of 'education' for very young children. She needs opportunities for exploration rather than tasks to fulfil.

And she does not have to be mentally or physically active all day. Time and peace, a sense of love and being loved —and just being and feeling — are equally essential to your baby's development as a rounded person.

*There was so much to learn that could only be absorbed through touch and experience. Lee studied every aspect of how a ball rolls . . .*

*. . . and found that a balloon may look like a ball but it weighs much less.*

*He discovered the sweet smell of a flower . . .*

*. . . and was intrigued to find his familiar world quite changed when viewed through a mesh.*

*Water, the cheapest and most varied play element, was a source of delight, satisfaction and exploration, from his first efforts at pouring and his early pleasure in bubbles through to quite complex experiments when he was two and three with funnels, sieves and flowerpots.*

*All his play could be ascribed to different aspects of learning or self-expression: for instance, a psychologist would look upon the bear as symbolizing Lee's mother when he cuddled it.*

# NEW ACHIEVEMENTS

At the end of your toddler's first year, her use of objects and toys will change subtly. Previously she will have been mostly interested in how they feel, smell or respond to her touch; now she will begin to enjoy making things work.

She has an in-built will to master a simple challenge. The provision of two or three suitable learning toys, together with gentle encouragement and praise, will cultivate her natural ambition.

It is worth putting together a box with a variety of toys and household bits and pieces to keep her busy and happy in her play-pen or at your feet as you work. There's certainly no need to spend a fortune on play equipment.

(However, larger equipment in the long run can be a worthwhile investment if space allows. A small, inflatable playpool provides the perfect base for every form of water play; a sand-pit also has endless possibilities. Best of all, in or out of doors, is a climbing frame with a slide; it not only encourages physical development, but is the perfect base – house, fortress, garage, anything – when your child reaches the stage of imaginative play.)

*Having the dexterity to cope with more than one thing at a time was a sign that he was reaching this next stage. His parents were enchanted with his triumph when at last he succeeded in banging two bricks together (their pleasure in his new trick diminished as his experiments grew noisier, especially once he had discovered saucepan lids).*

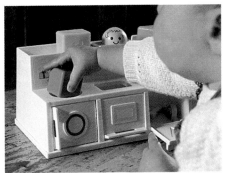

*Pulling a toy on wheels was another skill that took a while to master.*

*Learning toys became an enthralling challenge. He hardly needed to be taught how to use them. They were so cleverly designed that they brought out his innate instinct to achieve.*

*Only when a toy was slightly too difficult for him (so that he could see what should be done but just could not manage it) did he collapse in frustration. Then his mother would put the toy aside for a short while, until he was ready to try again more patiently.*

*However, he was dangerously successful in unscrewing a bottle-top at fourteen months. (This is supposed to be impossible before about two years.)*

# EARLY CREATIVITY

Creativity must be one of the most important aspects of development in ensuring your child's future happiness and success, both in recreation and at work, just as much in business and science as in the arts.

Much of your baby's day will be spent in action and play, but, even up to the age of two and beyond, as much as twenty per cent of her waking hours may be occupied in quietly sitting and staring. This is not wasted time, but is considered to be an essential part of observing and learning about everything around her. Having some time to dream is also important for creativity.

You may notice that she will look about her less actively if she is constrained in a play-pen, high chair, cot or car-seat, a surprising fact not yet explained by researchers.

*Lee not only rapidly increased his skills with learning toys but soon he started to create new ways of using almost everything he laid his hands on.*

*Never mind that his instinct led him to 'invent' almost precisely the same ideas as almost every other baby. Putting bricks on top of one another, in his experience, was absolutely original.*

*Given a selection of bits and pieces, he would dream up his own uses for them. Long before he could say 'jug' or 'brick', he understood through his own experiments the concepts of fullness and being overloaded.*

*Until he could hold images or ideas in his memory, he could only react to what was in front of him, and play with the toys as he saw them at that moment: in the same way, he still whined with hunger because of the discomfort of his empty stomach, and not because he pictured delicious food in his imagination.*

*However, some time after his first birthday, his memory had developed enough to tell him that he'd seen a jug being used for pouring, and that it was rather like a mug; then he was ready and able to play his first game of 'Let's pretend . . .'*

# LEARNING THROUGH IMITATION

Your baby will instinctively imitate the actions of adults or older children – a very important factor in acquiring more advanced behaviour and skills, and, later, in agglomerating the basic ingredients for a fertile imagination.

*From very early on in his development, Lee had been unconsciously copying various movements of his parents, which became imprinted on his memory so that they became his own.*

*Perhaps the earliest obvious imitation was with the telephone, which so frequently seemed to share his mother's attention.*

*As his play skills increased, copying became fun . . .*

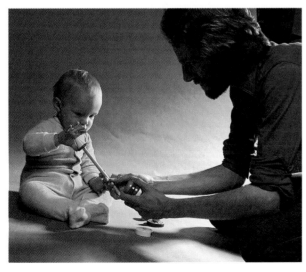

*. . . whether sharing a musical
instrument . . .*

*. . . a construction toy . . .*

*. . . or something more practical,
which involved useful learning as
well as amusement.*

# COPING WITH ABSTRACTS

*At around thirteen or fourteen months, Lee started consciously to relate one object to another in his mind. This was a big step forward from just bashing two things together to make a noise.*

*By copying the way his mother apparently 'played' with her 'toys', he recognized that the sweeper had some specific connection with the floor. Perhaps he could even see that his mother had some purpose in mind when she put them together – though he didn't yet understand what it was.*

*Through such experiences, he eventually understood that there were a whole lot of happenings that took place without him having to do anything himself: he could visualize the fact that people and objects continued to exist when he couldn't see them.*

*The recognition that other people had lives of their own, independent of his, made him even more interested in their actions. He wanted to imitate whatever his parents did, as well as his most admired character, the boy next door.*

*In his third year, he was less likely to try to solve problems by physical action: it was possible to see by the flickering on his face that thoughts were going through his mind.*

*Sometimes he could think out a solution: he could call to mind something that was in another room, find it and take it elsewhere for a practical purpose. For instance, at two and a half, he appeared in the kitchen with a chair, so that he could climb up beside his father to share the splashy bubbles of the washing-up.*

# DISCOVERING CONCEPTS THROUGH PLAY

Your child will gradually find out that many things are not at all what they seem. She only comes to understand new concepts as she gathers experience and develops her ability to think and to learn; it is more a matter of curiosity and maturity than of teaching or explanation.

For instance, once she has mastered the idea of 'large' and 'small', she will gradually develop a concept of 'more' and 'less'. Some time later, you might present her with a small glass filled to the brim with water and a tall glass partly filled with the same amount of water, and ask which has 'more' in it. At first, she will tell you that the full glass has more in it than the half-empty one. Only when she has enough experience of pouring and checking as well as the maturity to enjoy and make sense of this play, will she produce the correct answer.

Probably the hardest concept to grasp is *time*. When is 'soon', and will 'tomorrow' ever come? And how long is 'Wait!'?

*At only eight months, Lee discovered by experience the difference between three- and two-dimensional objects: after a session grabbing daisies in the garden he tried to pick the flowers out of the carpet.*

*The stream of water looked as solid as a curtain or a piece of string; he had to learn the concept that pouring liquid cannot be held.*

*He later became confused, believing anything that moved to be alive; at one stage he was scared by the seed heads he himself had blown from the dandelion.*

*And he simply could not recognize his hero-worshipped friend from next door, altered only by an insubstantial wig.*

*Even at the age of three, if he could not see his father, he thought he was successfully hiding from him.*

# DRAWING AND WRITING

The instinct to make one's mark goes back to primitive man; as soon as your baby can grip a crayon comfortably, she will want to make use of it – not always on the most appropriate surfaces!

Definite left- or right-handedness usually becomes apparent early on, but may confirm itself only in your child's third year. Life is slightly easier for right-handed people, owing to the design of, for example, scissors or some sports equipment.

Left-handedness usually stems from the neurological connection between your child's brain and her arm and hand, and it will probably harm her rather than help her if you try to interfere. Many outstanding academics, great sportsmen and talented artists (including Michelangelo) have been left-handed – so there is no need to worry one way or the other.

*Lee's progress in using crayons was typical of many aspects of child development in that it emphasized his need to mature both mentally and physically before certain achievements would be possible.*

*At nine months, when his mother drew a simple diagram for him to copy, his fist was still too clumsy to manipulate the crayon: though he wanted whatever she had in her hand, he was more interested in scrunching up the paper.*

*Months later, when she drew a square, he had enough control over his hand to manipulate the crayon, but instinctively covered the paper in wide sweeps rather than attempting a copy of her diagram.*

*Around the age of two, he could recognize her drawing of, for example, a truck; however, he would only try to copy when she showed him a simple pattern.*

*He mostly used his right hand for finer actions, but seemed almost equally skilful with the left when it suited him.*

*He was not only interested in what adults regarded as the 'correct use' for a crayon, but also needed to explore its other possibilities.*

*Eventually he was ready to copy, even some letters of the alphabet, though he did not understand what they represented. (Because of the similar, clearly shaped letters of his name, he could more or less write it before he could draw a representational picture of any sort.)*

# FROM IMITATION TO IMAGINATION

In your child's third year, dolls and toy animals really come into their own, peopling her imaginary situations as she re-lives and re-plays her version of the confusing grown-up world around her.

A dressing-up box containing old scarves and hats, and any unwanted garments (the more colourful and flowing, the better), will be a rich source of happiness, helping her games of pretend. She will also need plenty of picture books, and frequent trips to the library.

Ideally she could have her own enclosed space – a Wendy House or a climbing frame (which has so many other uses too), or some sort of home-made screen, possibly with a window cut into it so that she doesn't feel shut in, yet is secure in her own corner to let her imagination fly.

The development of your child's imagination can be seen in her ability to use things in her own way (as opposed to copying); this is the beginning of her having her own ideas. It is the basis of her future creativity – a vital ingredient for a happy and fulfilling life.

*Lee's game of spooning food into his parents' mouths had been mere imitation. It was a different matter when he reached the stage of ordering his monkey to eat a banana: he'd never seen anyone feeding a toy, so this action involved real imagination.*

*Indeed, he was no longer just copying his parents; completely absorbed, and muttering to himself, he was imagining that he actually was his own father doing the ironing . . .*

... and felt as if he was his mother doing the crossword.

His imaginative play sometimes reflected aggravations in his own life. When playing with his toy town, he found deep satisfaction in manipulating the miniature people, in making them carry out actions and putting them where he wanted: this made him feel just like his mother and other gigantic adults who could move him about at will, and take him off to bed in the middle of a game.

He still enjoyed the same sort of toys – trucks, bricks, dolls, household objects – but he played with more intensity and in a more complex way. In his imagination, a climbing frame became a house when required, and a plateful of flower petals from the garden became a meal for a 'visitor' (in the form of the old teddy bear).

# ON TO THE FUTURE

There is nothing truer than the old adage that 'play is children's work'. However, your child does not have to be using her mind all the time. Physical activities provide another sort of learning: about balance, control and speed. Equally important are the quiet moments – love, peace and having time to dream and think.

While ensuring that this vital equilibrium is achieved, it is fascinating to watch the way your child's play now helps her towards a more sophisticated degree of understanding. Counting, categorizing, simple measuring and naming colours are typically useful skills which contribute to giving her a headlong start at school; and the habit of being observant will stand her in good stead for her whole life. In her pre-school years, she is constantly absorbing more and more knowledge, but creatively rather than drily, through play rather than through imposed lessons.

Only if she is insecure, hurting with jealousy of a new baby, or hedged in by a barrage of 'No!' and 'Don't!' and 'Be quiet!', is she likely to curl up into herself, unable to progress normally.

But if she is confident, she will naturally want to please, to share her delight with you in all her small triumphs. That she feels happy, secure, loved and admired by her parents will be the rock-strong basis from which she can later comfortably learn whatever she needs.

*In Lee's third year, it became possible to see, for instance in the way he played with water, just how instinctive 'experiments' were building up his knowledge. (Even the most brilliant physicist has to go through these early stages, developing the skill to pour, starting to understand volume, weight and overflow and the density of different liquids.) Water, the cheapest play material, probably offers the most educational opportunities.*

*Aged three, Lee still explored the physical characteristics of everything new he came across, but his discoveries were more interesting. Indeed, it could be seen as another small step* *towards understanding hydro-electricity when he created ripples in the bird-bath and watched enthralled as they circled outwards.*

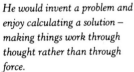

*He would invent a problem and enjoy calculating a solution – making things work through thought rather than through force.*

*Meanwhile he had gradually learned to categorize and sort: round from square, one colour from another – then more refined distinctions, things that looked different yet belonged to the same group. He was fascinated, for example, by the variety of types of brushes: for teeth, for hair, for painting or for house-cleaning. He happily spent long periods sorting things that are so obvious to adults that they forget that children have to learn to make distinctions. These games were fun, part of his natural urge to make more sense of the world around him.*

*He had also started to count: 'one', 'two' and 'three' (though 'three' at that age usually meant 'many'). Just as important, however, was the joy of sploshing on paint and achieving colourful results. And even more vital was the accompanying praise from his parents which helped him to bask in a positive self-image.*

# FIRST ENCOUNTERS

Your baby will enjoy the presence of other children and sense a certain comradeship long before she is ready to play with them constructively. The company of her own generation is an important stimulus, especially if she has no brothers or sisters.

In the first two years, because she is still 'egocentric' – the centre of her own world – and unable to know how others feel, she is likely to grab toys from a contemporary, or to explore his eyes, which she sees as attractive, shiny baubles.

Some experts say that a doll or a teddy bear is a better companion in the first two years because your baby can explore embroidered eyes or plastic-jointed arms without doing any damage. However, with alert supervision, two babies are not likely to do each other any serious harm, and it seems a pity to deprive them of this early human contact which they plainly enjoy.

*Lee's mother had made several friends both in hospital and later at the baby clinic. They were all in similar situations, and had much to talk about – but their babies at first only saw one another in the same way as they would a new teddy bear or toy, as interesting objects to investigate.*

*Though he was too young to play, Lee was definitely intrigued by his own generation; his broadest smiles were for the older children next door.*

*Edward was his most frequent companion. By the time they could sit comfortably side by side, they seemed to recognize each other, and both found plenty to stare at in the other's behaviour.*

*Babies, even toddlers, are said to play 'in parallel' rather than co-operatively. However, at ten months, Lee and Edward were developing a rather exceptional relationship, and their 'parallel' play often took account of each other's activity.*

*Tania was another regular visitor, though peace between her and Lee did not always last long.*

*Like most girls, she was more advanced than her male contemporaries: she walked earlier, had a stronger will, and usually gained the upper hand. She was not rough on purpose – she was too young to understand that she could hurt someone else, or to imagine what it felt like on the receiving end.*

# DEVELOPING SOCIAL SKILLS

*Lee's first birthday party (and his second) was enjoyed more by the parents than by the children, who were still at an age when they were happiest playing in pairs. In a group they became submerged in uncertainty.*

*Though Lee appreciated his regular few friends, he was not interested in children whom he did not know. It was his passion for everything on wheels rather than his increasing sociability that caused him to make off in the park with a challengingly awkward buggy that happened to be loaded with somebody else's baby. (The mother made quite a scene.)*

*For a long time the children still unconsciously played 'parallel' to one another. Lee and Andrew were sometimes almost like two dancers, reflecting each other's movements.*

*They also went in for a certain amount of smash and grab, being too young to understand about sharing . . .*

*. . . but gradually they also showed signs of real co-operation.*

# REAL FRIENDS

To flourish at playgroup and later at school, your child will need not only to be able to use her brain and to enjoy sport: it is just as valuable – throughout life – that she can make friends readily and hold her own in a group.

Your part in helping her learn to get on with others is very important. You are her first companion, and she learns most of her attitudes to others through her relationship with you, especially if she has no brothers or sisters. One way you can help her to develop satisfactory social contacts with her own generation is to avoid being dominant when you play with her yourself. When she's ready, let her take the initiative, be the 'leader', have her own ideas. And you have to find the difficult balance, never abandoning her to the mercy of other children who are accidentally rough, yet at the same time resisting the natural, loving temptation to be over-protective.

Your child will find it much easier to form true friendships if she has had plenty of early opportunities to share play, even to take a few knocks from her contemporaries, as she meets them both at home and at mother-and-toddler groups.

*Once the children had developed a certain amount of speech, their friendships grew into true companionship.*

*They were able to work out aggressions in imaginative games. Both Tania and Lee were plunged into jealousy of younger sisters at about the same time; they took it in turns to play the baby and the bossy adult, and this seemed to help them simmer down emotionally.*

They learnt from each other, and put their heads together in their attempts to solve problems.

They also enjoyed the company of older children.

They seemed to practise, each in turn, to take the lead.

Lee's friends were a very important part of his life.

# INDEX